WALK A *Different* PATH

THOUGHTS FROM THE JOURNEY

RYAN GARRISON

Walk a Different Path: A Collection of Thoughts
Trilogy Christian Publishers A Wholly Owned Subsidiary of Trinity Broadcasting Network

2442 Michelle Drive Tustin, CA 92780

Copyright © 2024 by Ryan Garrison

Scripture quotations marked ESV are taken from the ESV® Bible (The Holy Bible, English Standard Version®), copyright © 2001 by Crossway Bibles, a publishing ministry of Good News Publishers. ©All rights reserved. Scripture quotations marked NKJV are taken from the New King James Version®. Copyright © 1982 by Thomas Nelson. Used by permission. All rights reserved. Scripture quotations marked NLT are taken from the Holy Bible, New Living Translation, copyright © 1996, 2004, 2015 by Tyndale House Foundation. Used by permission of Tyndale House Publishers, Inc., Carol Stream, Illinois 60188. All rights reserved. Scripture quotations marked KJV are taken from the King James Version of the Bible. Public domain.

No part of this book may be reproduced, stored in a retrieval system, or transmitted by any means without written permission from the author. All rights reserved. Printed in the USA.

Rights Department, 2442 Michelle Drive, Tustin, CA 92780.

Trilogy Christian Publishing/TBN and colophon are trademarks of Trinity Broadcasting Network.

For information about special discounts for bulk purchases, please contact Trilogy Christian Publishing.

Trilogy Disclaimer: The views and content expressed in this book are those of the author and may not necessarily reflect the views and doctrine of Trilogy Christian Publishing or the Trinity Broadcasting Network.

10 9 8 7 6 5 4 3 2 1

Library of Congress Cataloging-in-Publication Data is available.

ISBN: 979-8-89333-201-8
E-ISBN: 979-8-89333-202-5

ACKNOWLEDGMENTS

To my loving Savior, Jesus Christ, who not only died for me, but inspires me to be the best person I can be. The One who sees me struggle and fall, yet who gently lifts me back up with His loving hands and comforts me in every situation in which I seem to find myself.

To my late wife, Renae, the love I didn't deserve. You are the best person I have ever known and the most amazing wife and mother we could have ever hoped for. Your spirit of love and kindness lives on forever through us.

To my children: Connor, Chloe, and Matthew—three of the most incredible little humans that any dad could have asked for. Your love and sweet spirits inspire me to be the best daddy I can be.

To my siblings: Chris, Amber, and Andrea. We have had some great moments and some tragic ones, but the bond between us is unbreakable. When I think of each of you, I know God has blessed me more than I truly deserve, because we are family.

To my many friends who have inspired me to put this into print, thank you for your support and faith in me to allow God to use His gift through one as undeserving as I.

Finally, to you, the reader. These are my thoughts, which God has given me, and I hope that if one person who reads this comes to know our Father in a way that changes their life, then it has been worth every stroke of the keyboard. You are worth more than any precious jewel or amount of money—so much that the Creator chose to die rather than live without you.

FOREWORD

I have had several people ask me where the *Walk a Different Path* posts come from. In June 2020, I lost my wife, Renae, and then, in August, I also lost my mom. We had bought a house in Forney, and I was getting in the shower one day when I heard God tell me I was going to walk a different path. I had no idea what that was or how it would look, but I remember saying, "Your will be done." Fast-forward to a calm morning in November. I was sitting on my couch with Facebook open, staring out the window watching the fountain in the pool, when I started typing about what I saw. Before I knew it, the first post was completed—and it was then I realized it was my mom's birthday, as well.

I believe in my heart that we all have a purpose on this planet—or, as the song "My Testimony" from Elevation Worship, says, "If I'm not dead, then You're not done." I want these posts to be an encouragement to everyone who reads them, and it is my heart's desire that they lead you, the reader, to seek your Creator and Father, to accept a relationship with Him, one that moves mountains, one in which He crosses the expanse of space to meet you right where you are, reminding you of His love for you and how He longs to be with you. Jesus said, "I go to prepare a place . . ."—so can you imagine how wonderful a place that will be if He has been already spent two thousand years preparing it, just for you and me?

With this, I have been asked by several and many times to create a book or collection of these posts. I have been very hesitant to do so, because it's not about me in any way, but it's about reaching people and trying to be an instrument for His peace in any way I can. I truly love each of you, and I want so much for all the things you long for and hope for to be yours, but more importantly, I pray that you will know He loves you so much that He did not even spare what was most precious to Him. You are worth so much more than anything that has been created—more than any riches could ever buy. I have many wonderful friends who have reminded me that this is a ministry, not just random thoughts and writings, so thank you for reading.

Walk a Different Path.

TABLE OF CONTENTS

Part 1: The Path Begins 9
Part 2: Walking the Path 55
Part 3: The Journey Continues 97

Part 1
THE PATH BEGINS

Walk a different path.

I'm sitting here looking out the window, watching the calmness of the water in the pool. How many times has our calm been turned upside down? We lose someone, or we miss that deadline, or the kids get sick. It doesn't take much to interrupt the calm, and soon we have chaos in our hearts.

God specializes in remaining calm. He isn't surprised when things happen that are unexpected to us, things that make us anxious as our calm is unsettled. Jesus slept in the boat during the storm because He knew who was in control of the storm (see Luke 8:22–25). God will lead us through the storms that disrupt our calm days and hold our hand through it all.

Walk a different path. Keep calm—and maybe take a nap while the sea is rolling. God is in the storm.

#walkadifferentpath

Walk a different path.

We look at the world, see all the bad, and seem to forget that it is not the people, but the spirit behind it that is evil. We have forgotten what Paul warned us in Ephesians, and we seem to have missed that as we have become so wrapped up in our daily lives.

The souls of people are worth more than any amount of money. The war is not against that man or woman, but against the unseen forces, the spiritual forces in high places, that would seek to draw us away from God and destroy our souls. I know we may not always like people, but we have to remember that everyone is created in God's image and they are His creation, just like I am, just like you are. I will stand against those forces, for my children, for my family, for my friends, but most importantly, for my Savior. Let's bring a little honor back to what it means to be Christian—put on our armor and stand and fight.

Hate evil and love what is good; turn your courts into true halls of justice.

—Amos 5:15 NLT

Walk a different path. Show honor and know God sits on His throne.

#walkadifferentpath

Walk a different path.

Rejection and hopelessness can sometimes run hand in hand. We feel hopeless, so we reject the notion that someone could lift us up and truly care for us. We can be rejected by someone we care for, by our job, by our friends, and even by our family members, which can lead to the feeling that our lives are hopeless because no one wants us.

God is bigger than hopelessness. Our hope is in not who governs us, what job we have, or even who we are with. God has given us the hope that He will never leave us or forsake us. God is bigger than rejection. We may be rejected in this life—I sometimes call myself the "broken toy no one wants" . . . just kidding—but God will never reject us. He welcomes us into His Kingdom and makes us heirs to that Kingdom. We are not broken toys in His eyes.

Walk a different path. See your hope and acceptance in our Father's arms and know you are an heir to the Kingdom of God (see Psalm 78:7).

#walkadifferentpath

Walk a different path.

I'm sitting here thinking about birthdays. My twins turned five today, and their mom is not here to share in the celebration. It seems like yesterday when I took her to the hospital, and they came home with us the next day. What a joyous day that was—and now, five years later, she is gone, the kids are without their mom, and I am a widower.

Where is God in all of this? Why am I not angry? The simple truth is that God is in the midst of our pain, reaching into our hearts and souls and reminding us to lean on Him. Life here on earth is just a path that we all must take to get to our forever home. How can I be mad at that? Renae is there now and experiencing wonders I can't even fathom. She reached the end of her path and has walked into her forever home.

Walk a different path. God is waiting for you at the end (see Revelation 21:3).

#walkadifferentpath

Walk a different path.

Today is Veterans Day, and we should remember to thank the men and women who stand at attention as watchmen, guarding our freedom. Many times, their job is thankless, and they rush into places many will not go. I am forever grateful for their service.

There is another act of bravery and sacrifice that protected our freedom, and more importantly our souls. Nothing could ever measure up to the sacrifice that Jesus made on the cross of Calvary. With His death, we were set free from the prison of sin in which we had lived. His love for us proved more powerful than death, hell, and the grave.

Walk a different path. Thank a soldier for his or her service and sacrifice, but remember to also thank God for His Son's sacrifice and redeeming death (see Romans 5:7–8).

#walkadifferentpath

Walk a different path.

Loneliness. It's one of the roots of depression and despair. We all walk along in our lives, hoping to make connections with family, friends, and maybe even someone with whom you can spend the rest of your life. But what happens when family and friends are not there, or the man or woman you love leaves? Such a pit can develop in your heart and drag you down.

When loneliness comes, rely on His grace and love. Remember that you are never truly alone because God will carry your heart in His and make you feel alive again. God will take ninety-nine steps out of one hundred to reach you—you just have to take that last step toward Him. God is a gentleman, and His Spirit will comfort us if we allow Him to.

Walk a different path. You weren't meant to walk in loneliness, but in His abiding love.

#walkadifferentpath

Walk a different path.

It's Friday the thirteenth. I see so many posts about this date. Some people believe there is a curse on this day; other people believe it is unlucky—all because of a series of movies. No one thinks a masked killer will come out of a lake to attack them (or at least I hope they don't!), but this day still tends to fill people with dread and uneasiness.

God is not fazed by a date on our calendar. He is not fazed by anything, as He knows all things. God is the same yesterday, today, and forever. He is the Alpha and Omega, the Beginning and the End (see Revelation 1:8). And because He is all these things, we can face our past, today, and our future, knowing He is walking beside us, even when it doesn't feel like it.

Walk a different path. God is in control and still on His throne, and He does not hide His eyes from scary movies or superstitious dates.

#walkadifferentpath

Walk a different path.

Sometimes life can strain us, and we want to run and hide, locking ourselves away from the world. We weep bitter tears, or we have so many things that seem rational run through our heads that it can drive us crazy. We don't think anyone will "catch" us in our solitude and pain, so we feel more at home when we hide.

God is there in those moments when we want to hide, and He sees the pain, the tears, and the anguish we are going through. He reaches His hand down to comfort us. David said it best when he wrote in the Psalms: "Where can I go from Your Spirit, where can I [hide] from Your presence?" (Psalm 139:7 NKJV). Simply put, there is not a place that is too far, too lonely, or too much of a mess where God cannot lift you up.

Walk a different path. He is calling out in your dark room. Listen and run to Him with open arms.

#walkadifferentpath

Walk a different path.

Oftentimes we want something so badly that our very hearts ache for it. It could be that someone special, or maybe you long for kids, a new job, or healing in your body. It could be a number of things. But when we don't get it, we can feel our hearts break inside us. Love, being a parent, being happy and healthy—all are noble aspirations, but we can feel defeated when we don't obtain them.

God understands our heartache for the things we want. He understands that in this life no one wants to be alone, that we all long to be happy. In His infinite wisdom, He calls to us for Him to be our Source of joy, and He will supply our needs. He loves us better than any partner, He is the best parent, and He longs to heal our hearts from any hurt.

Walk a different path. Listen to the call of our Father and trust Him with your desires. He delights in giving His children what they need (see John 16:24).

#walkadifferentpath

Walk a different path.

Starting over. Moving on. Beginning anew. These can be scary words after the death of a loved one, the loss of a job, moving to a different city. The anxiety and stress is enough to make you lose sleep, worry about everything, and even feel like you are drowning.

God never intended life to be this way. He takes our hand and sometimes even carries us through these difficult times. Have you lost someone you love? He is the resurrection and the life. Have you lost your job? He opens doors no man can shut and shuts doors no man can open (see Revelation 3:7). God loves us so much that if we allow Him to, He will show us a path through our pain and worry to a better tomorrow.

Walk a different path. Let the God of creation be your Source and stand back and let Him work (see Isaiah 41:10).

#walkadifferentpath

Walk a different path.

Captain America. Such a hero to me. Go ahead and laugh, but as I was growing up, he helped instill in me the honor I still carry to this day. His sense of doing what was right, no matter what it cost, is ingrained into my very soul.

Cap may be a fictional character, but the God we serve isn't. God wants us to always do what is right and whatever is holy, whatever is honorable. To seek out evil and put a stop to it. To love Him and serve Him when everyone around us is mocking us. That is true honor. It should be carried in our relationships with Him, with our partners, our family members, and our friends.

Walk a different path. God is deserving of honor, and He will honor us if we follow His ways (see Micah 6:8).

#walkadifferentpath

Walk a different path.

Sacrifice. We see this in the world so much. A soldier laying down his life for his country, a single parent doing whatever they can to make sure their child is happy and cared for, or a police officer or fireman risking his life for others. Sacrifice happens around us all the time, but we don't often recognize it.

Two thousand years ago, the most courageous sacrifice took place on a hill called Calvary. Jesus took a savage beating, was mocked and spit on, then was literally nailed to a cross. His crime? Nothing. God allowed this to take place so that heaven could be open to us. What other God can boast such a claim as this?

Walk a different path. God's sacrifice of His Son was made so that we could know the joy of spending eternity with Him (see Romans 5:7–8).

#walkadifferentpath

Walk a different path.

What does it mean to keep going? To persevere, to stick it out, or to just dust ourselves off and get back in the race. It seems like every day something comes our way and causes us to stumble, trip, or fall entirely.

God calls us to persevere in all trials. Jesus is the perfect example in that He knows what it is like to be tired. (Remember the nap He took in the boat?) He knows what it is like to be thirsty. (Does His drink at the well with Samaritan woman ring a bell?) And He knows what it is like to suffer. The point is that through it all, He persevered and left us an example of how we should always put God's will first in our lives over our own, for that is how we will make it through this life.

Walk a different path. To him that overcomes, He will give the crown of life (see 1 John 5:5).

#walkadifferentpath

Walk a different path.

It's hard to accept that things change, but they do. Loved ones leave or pass away, careers change, and kids grow up. Such changes can lead us to be anxious or worried and start to question what life means.

God understands. This is why He said to "be anxious for nothing" (Philippians 4:6 NKJV). He sees our worries and empathizes with us as a Father would. There is nothing that surprises Him, nothing that catches Him off guard. If He knows what lies ahead, we should be able to lean on Him and trust that He has a firm hand on our lives and wants to give us His best.

Walk a different path. God is the God of change, but He always allows things to happen for our benefit.

#walkadifferentpath

Walk a different path.

Resentment. Bitterness's twin sister. We can come to resent many things. The loss of a loved one, friends we feel betrayed us, or family whom we feel has deserted us. No matter what we feel, however, resentment can take root and slowly introduce your heart to her sister, bitterness. And once you meet them and invite them in, they can be hard to kick back out of your heart.

God doesn't want us to wallow in resentment or bitterness, because He knows where that path will lead (see Hebrews 12:15). God teaches us that the heart can deceive us and lead us to bitterness, but through His love we can break that chain and live the life He has called us to live. His Word tells us that it is He who has kept our soul from the pit of nothingness.

Walk a different path. Forgive as He forgave you so that the twins of resentment and bitterness will not take root in your life.

#walkadifferentpath

Walk a different path.

We long for that relationship, for that job promotion, and even sometimes for that child whom we have wanted and waited for. We can long for something so much that in the very depths of our souls, we feel our hearts may explode—because what we long for is true and virtuous in our eyes.

God understands, and that is why there is hope. Hope is the trinity of what it means to love. Faith and love are its inseparable sisters, and God specializes in giving hope. Hope teaches us to hold on one more day, to have the courage to take a leap and trust Him when all else seems to be against us. Hope can never be extinguished because God cannot be.

Walk a different path. Hope just a little longer, because God honors a hopeful heart (see Psalm 38:15).

#walkadifferentpath

Walk a different path.

"Remember your chains." I heard this from a Christian singer years ago, and I have always found it to speak to my soul. Remembering what you have been through and facing those chains that used to keep you down can be hard sometimes. With all that life throws at us, remembering can sometimes feel like an anchor weighing us down.

But this is not how God intended remembering. As the song says, remember your chains—but also remember your chains are gone. God removes those things that held us back from a deeper fulfillment of His love and grace. He allows us to remember those chains, however, so we can truly see how far He has brought us (see Philippians 3:13–14).

Walk a different path. Imagine what your life would be if Jesus had not set you free.

#walkadifferentpath

Walk a different path.

At Thanksgiving, I take time to reflect and think about all I am thankful for. I love to spend time with family in laughter, remembering those who are no longer here, with loved ones close by to make the day brighter.

God loves our thanksgiving (see 1 Thessalonians 5:18). He loves hearing us say, "Thank You for all You do." He rejoices when His children reach out in praise and tell Him we are thankful that He is our Source. What a beautiful love story there is between man and his Creator.

Walk a different path. Give thanks with a grateful heart, because He has given all we could ever need.

#walkadifferentpath

Walk a different path.

What does it mean to trust? To give your heart to someone and believe they will always have your back, no matter what? What happens when that trust is broken—or worse, taken advantage of? Can trust ever be restored?

God treats our trust as a sacred thing, as a holy covenant with Him. We can trust Him to always do what is right in our lives because of His love for us (see Psalm 31:14). He demonstrated this love at the cross of Cavalry. By allowing Jesus to go through the pain and then the resurrection, God was telling us, "You can trust Me. I will never leave you nor forsake you."

Walk a different path. Trust in the One who knows your heart and who takes that into account in your relationship with Him. He never fails.

#walkadifferentpath

Walk a different path.

How do we know what the right thing is? How can we tell what is the proper path we should take? How can live life while so aware that we may slip and fall, that someone may break our heart, or that life may just be too hard? How can we move forward in such uncertainty?

God knows all (see Psalm 1:6). He sees things through the eyes that see eternity. He knows what is right, because He is right and just. He knows what the proper path is because He sees them all. Will we slip and fall, will other people hurt us, or will life ever weigh us down? Possibly, but He is faithful to show up just in time to tell us in His still, small voice, "I've got you" (see John 14:18).

Walk a different path. Don't just *hope* that God has you in His arms—*know* that He does.

#walkadifferentpath

Walk a different path.

Revenge is a slippery slope. Too often we feel that we have been wronged and we need to get back at the one who offended us. We feel they deserve to feel the hurt and pain that we have gone through, and sometimes we will not stop until we see "justice" (see Romans 12:19).

This is not the life God intends for us to live. He knows the slippery slope that is vengeance, and He asks us to forgive, even when it seems too hard to do so. God seeks to give us a life free from the bitterness that forms when we feel we have been wronged or hurt, by showing us the ultimate sign of forgiveness at the cross of Cavalry.

Walk a different path. Choose life so that you might live, and forgive so that your soul can be free.

#walkadifferentpath

Walk a different path.

Brotherhood or sisterhood. Is there any greater feeling than to know that someone has your back? That there is a bond between you and those particular people in your life whom you feel cannot be broken. That no matter what happens, you know they will be there to pick you up, standing back to back with you and helping you fight?

God knew what He was doing when He commanded we love our neighbor as ourselves (see Matthew 22:39). He knew that if we loved each other, then that feeling of having each other's backs would be amplified. By loving Him and cascading that love down to others, the bonds of brotherhood/sisterhood could not be easily broken.

Walk a different path. Let God's love flow and strengthen the bonds between us.

#walkadifferentpath

Walk a different path.

Joy is so freeing. It allows us to forget the daily grind of life and lets our hearts and souls fly free. Sometimes it is hard to see the joy in the everyday battles and struggles we go through, and our laughter can be dimmed or even extinguished altogether.

God loves to hear us express our joy (see Psalm 32:11). He takes joy in the happiness that we share with others and in everyday life. God has given each of us a spirit deep inside that longs for the utter joy of knowing Him, which in turn allows us to share that joy with others.

Walk a different path. Let your light shine in all that you do and remember to keep joy in your heart.

#walkadifferentpath

Walk a different path.

They run into the building that's on fire. They patrol the streets when they are hated. They serve our country abroad, even if they don't agree with why they are there. Firemen, police officers, and soldiers. The very epitome of courage and bravery.

God tells us to be brave and of good courage. We might not run into the fire or fight in a war, but the courage God wants us to have is not necessarily demonstrated in those things, but rather it is shown in the everyday life we face. To stand against evil and do what is right, no matter the cost, is a true sign of godly courage, and it is how we honor Him.

Walk a different path. Courage is not the absence of fear, but action in spite of it (see Deuteronomy 31:6).

#walkadifferentpath

Walk a different path.

We have seen them on the television. Amazing displays of strength in lifting weights. We have read the stories of when a man or woman had supernatural strength and could overcome all the odds. How many of us have seen that strength fail when things got rough, or when bad news happened? We don't live in a fairy-tale world where everything gets neatly wrapped at the end of the story and the hero/heroine overcomes all the obstacles with their great strength.

God gives us physical gifts, but it is the strength of heart and character that matters the most (see Joshua 1:7). The true measure of a person is the strength in their heart. To go the extra mile, to hold on one more day, to do the right thing—against all odds. These things are more important to Him than how much physical weight we can lift.

Walk a different path. You are stronger than you know, because your Creator grants the grace and mercy needed to strengthen your heart and soul.

#walkadifferentpath

Walk a different path.

That amazing sunrise, or even the sunset. The laughter of a child playing. The smile of a person you love. All these things can cause our hearts to overflow and skip a beat. The beauty of this world and the people and things in it can overwhelm us with emotion.

God is the Author of beauty. We only have to take a deep look around to see His hand in all things. He created the waterfalls, the stars, even the air we breathe, but the most beautiful thing He created was each of us, and His love for His creation is why Calvary is so important—for He would die to have you with Him.

Walk a different path. See the beauty God has created in you and know that you are beautiful to Him (see 1 Peter 3:4).

#walkadifferentpath

Walk a different path.

How many times has the alarm clock gone off and you thought, *No, it's too soon!* Or the kids are screaming and arguing, and your mind cries out, *Why?* Life can come at you fast, and before you know it, you feel like you are on a carousel that someone turned to 100 and you are gripping with all your might just to hang on.

God has the answer for all the noise in our lives; it's called peace. The peace that passes all understanding (see Philippians 4:7). The still, small voice in the storms of life that whispers, *It's okay, I've got you.* No one can grant peace like God can, because only He knows what will calm our hearts.

Walk a different path. Listen for His voice and rest your mind, heart, and soul.

#walkadifferentpath

Walk a different path.

Someday is my favorite word in the dictionary. Someday I will see my kids grow up. Someday I will pay my house off. This word has so much power in it, yet someday can be a burden to many people. *When will my someday come? Why hasn't my someday come?* We often question these things, and when it seems they are not coming, someday turns to sorrow.

God specializes in someday. Sarah prayed that someday she would have a child—and behold Isaac. Israel prayed for deliverance—and behold Moses. Shadrach, Meshach, and Abednego believed God could save them from the fiery furnace—and the fire did not burn. Mary and Joseph were obedient—and Jesus was born. Saul walked the road and was blinded—and then there was Paul. God uses our hopes for someday, and then gives us our someday when we need it—at just the right time (see Galatians 4:4).

Walk a different path. Someday is coming, and when it does, you will not long for any other day.

#walkadifferentpath

Walk a different path.

One of my all-time favorite movies is *Hacksaw Ridge*. After seeing his friend die, the lead character asks, "What is it you want from me? I don't understand. I can't hear you." Desmond is asking this due to all the chaos around him and the uncertainty of the life waiting for him at home. He has seen death all around him, and he is now asking God why he can't hear Him.

Perseverance in the face of uncertainty and despair is not something man can do alone. God grants us strength and peace when life knocks us down and it seems we will never be able to get back up. God is calling out to our souls, and He says, *Keep going, I am with you.* It's in our weakness that He is made strong (see 1 Corinthians 1:25; Ephesians 6:10).

Walk a different path. To him who overcomes, He will give the crown of life.

#walkadifferentpath

Walk a different path.

You see it all the time. Man struggles and wrestles with his conscience on whether to intervene, or say something, for fear of how he or she will be perceived by the masses. We allow that which is wrong to become the norm, and then we react negatively when the payment for our complacency comes due.

God expects us to always do what is right (see Deuteronomy 6:18). He expects us to help the weak, defend the helpless, and be kind to each other. To be that light that will shine in someone's darkness, and to never back down when things get hard. Doing the right thing is never the hardest thing to do, and God honors those who will stand when all others fall away.

Walk a different path. All evil needs to prosper is for good men to do nothing.

#walkadifferentpath

Walk a different path.

These eyes have seen it, and this heart has even felt it a few times. It comes in, and we don't see it sometimes until it is too late. There are some times when it is okay, but most of the time, it is very destructive to our minds, hearts, and souls. What is this little troublemaker that can lower even the most powerful ruler?

God resists the proud. I don't mean pride in a job well done or that your child has accomplished something. The kind of pride God hates is when we puff out our chests and say, "I can do this all on my own," or "I don't need anyone, especially God." Pride is probably the sin God hates the most because it takes root in our hearts and affects every other thing around us (see James 4:6). God wants us to humble ourselves and not be prideful because He loves us and knows the cost that pride has on our souls.

Walk a different path. Avoid the fall.

#walkadifferentpath

Walk a different path.

I am going to work hard so I can buy that new car. Oh man, I love how that house looks, and it just fits our needs. That girl is so pretty, I am going to talk to her and try to win her heart. Pursuit. We are so focused on the things we want, what will satisfy us, that we are willing to pursue those things without question. While there is nothing wrong with wanting to obtain a car, house, or significant other, it is the sense that it overcomes us that we should be wary of.

God understands our needs and wants, as well as our pursuit of these things (see James 4:2). God wants to shelter us, and He wants us to feel fulfilled; however, that fulfillment comes from our relationship with Him. Think about this: We pursue all these things that can fade away at any time, but the very Creator of the universe pursues each and every one of us with His love. He loves us so much that He was willing to sacrifice the most precious thing to Him, just in the pursuit of you and me.

Walk a different path. Let your heart and soul be pursued by the One who matters and fall in love with Him all over again.

#walkadifferentpath

Walk a different path.

"I am so sorry. What can I do to make it better?" "How did it come to this, and what do I have to do to prove that I didn't mean to hurt you?" Most of us will do things in our lives that scar someone else, and we will seek forgiveness—or better said, redemption—for what we have done. The Spirit speaks to us in the darkest hours of the night and reminds us that something is wrong and it needs to be fixed.

God is in the redemption business. He specializes in taking broken hearts and making them whole. And while there may be consequences or penalties for actions we have taken, He promises to lead and guide us through those times in our walk, to be redeemed and sit with Him in glory. There is no depth to which He will not go to redeem a wounded soul.

Walk a different path. Cry out to Him who has redeemed us with the blood spilled at Calvary (see Psalm 18:6).

#walkadifferentpath

Walk a different path.

A cold hand touches our hearts from time to time. This unseen thing will cause our minds to run in so many different circles that we feel that no matter what we do, we can't seem to shake it. It comes in, grabs hold of us, and sometimes can shake us to our very core. Regret: the silent but crippling cousin of despair.

God knows we will sometimes allow what we should have done or said haunt us and that we will let regret take hold in our lives. God wants us to be regretful of things we have said and done, because remorse leads to repentance, and repentance to forgiveness. True forgiveness can then lead to freedom. God did not call us to live a life full of regret, thinking about those things for which He has forgiven us (see 2 Corinthians 7:10).

Walk a different path. Shake off the shackles of regret. Let go and let God heal.

#walkadifferentpath

Walk a different path.

Truth is one of the rarest traits in today's world. Too many times, we hide the truth because we are afraid of someone finding out something we are doing or something we have done. We gloss over truth to meet our ends and to satisfy the need to not be held accountable.

God is truth, and He expects us to walk in the truth on a daily basis (see Psalm 15:1–2). He knows that walking in truth will illuminate the path before us and does not give evil the chance to take root in our lives. By walking in truth, we begin to see His wonderful persona and who He really is, a holy Father who loves us and wants the best for us.

Walk a different path. Seek the truth in all that you do and live a life free from fear.

#walkadifferentpath

Walk a different path.

The desire to achieve goals is admirable. It pushes us to work harder and stay the course to achieve those goals. However, desire can also lead us down some paths we were not meant to go. By wanting something so bad, or by wanting to see something happen, we can find ourselves lost in desire with no clear way out of it.

God knows we are all human and that we desire many things. His Word tells us to delight in Him and He will give us the desires of our hearts (see Psalm 37:4). God also knows that when we desire Him above all else, those promises He speaks of will be the culmination of our true desire to follow and love Him.

Walk a different path. Desire His presence in your life.

#walkadifferentpath

Walk a different path.

Failure is a debilitating problem for all of us. We feel like we are not good enough or that our efforts are not appreciated. We can become depressed and feel hopeless due to some failure we perceive as life-changing.

God understands we can feel like failures. He wants to take us by the hand and show us that failure is not the end, but rather, a lesson from which we can learn and grow. Some of the most influential people in the Bible can be looked at as failures, but God took them at their lowest moments and brought them up to victory.

Walk a different path. Failures are going to happen, but God's plan is anything but (see Psalm 73:26).

#walkadifferentpath

Walk a different path.

Have you ever seen a movie where a volcano erupts and spews lava high in the air? Or have you watched as an explosive device detonated and toppled a building? Most of us have seen this on television or in movie theaters, but this also happens in our everyday lives. Anger is the "volcano" or "explosions" in daily life, and like a natural disaster, it can cause so much harm and ruin in our lives.

God does not say we can't be angry, but He does say not to let it lead us to sin (see Psalm 4:4). He knows there are things in our lives that will make us angry—being passed over a certain promotion, having a friend desert us, or experiencing the loss of a loved one. God understands, and He wants us to use those times when we feel so angry to draw closer to Him so He can soothe our hearts and restore our souls.

Walk a different path. Do not let the sun go down on your anger and avoid the "explosions" in life (see Ephesians 4:26).

#walkadifferentpath

Walk a different path.

"In brightest day, in blackest night, no evil shall escape my sight." Those are the opening lines from the oath of the Green Lantern Corps. I know you might laugh, but this resounds with me because these heroes overcome their fear and serve the galaxy without regard to their own safety. I know it may be fictional, but there is still something about that statement that speaks to my soul.

God calls us to live a life without fear and to walk in His light (see John 8:12). He reminds us daily that like the oath declares, He is there in brightest day and our blackest nights, as well. He is that voice that strengthens us and gives us the will to carry on, even when we think we can't go any further. Nothing escapes His sight, and very soon justice will prevail over all the evil we see.

Walk a different path. Be overcomers of evil with the light of good.

#walkadifferentpath

Walk a different path.

How many times have you felt at the end of the line, or that you were at rock bottom? How hard it is to make it in this world, even to just basically survive. It seems that everywhere we look, someone is trying to sell something that will make life better, we get involved in a relationship to feel something positive, or we just stop trying and harden our hearts to everything around us.

God has a plan for all these things we see on a daily basis, but He asks for one thing from us—faith. Faith is so powerful in that it can move the mountains that are in front of us, it can withstand the storms that batter us, and it can calm our souls when we feel hardened by the hurt around us. Faith is the sister of Love and Hope, and it works itself into our lives and souls and tells us that God will never abandon us. The dust just needs to be brushed off as we get back up and stand tall.

Walk a different path. Faith is the evidence of things unseen (see Hebrews 11:11), and the unseen is coming to show you better days.

#walkadifferentpath

Walk a different path.

We look at things that happen in the world, and it doesn't seem to faze us. Have we become so indifferent to all that goes on around us? We see things that used to spark our hearts to action, but now there is just nothing—no sense of the absolute nature of right and wrong. We have become indifferent because we believe we can't change anything.

I am so glad David didn't feel that way. He took up the sling and challenged the giant. One rock later, and the enemy was fleeing. God uses us to challenge the indifference we see in the world, to challenge that which seems to crush our spirits and calls us to action, just like David (see 1 Samuel 17:50).

Walk a different path. Arm your heart with the Rock that is our salvation and shatter the window of indifference in your life.

#walkadifferentpath

Walk a different path.

After a few days, we are back at it again. Some days we run and run, faster and faster, not taking the time to slow down and enjoy life. Rest does not come because we are so worried about what is next on our to-do lists or the places we have to be.

God rested on the seventh day (see Genesis 2:2–3), not because He was tired from His work, but to set an example for us: we need to stop and rest, as well. Life can get so busy and complicated, and He wants us to remember that it is okay to rest from the day-to-day grind and just be at peace.

Walk a different path. Rest in the arms of your heavenly Father and let your burdens go.

#walkadifferentpath

Walk a different path.

It's everywhere you look. You can't see it, but you feel it every day in your life. Honestly, *sometimes* joyful, fulfilled lives can feel like a burden. It's a responsibility. And you can't run from it—it's always there. Many people try to escape it, but it shows up every time you think you have given it the slip.

A Christ-centered responsibility is instilled in all of us. We are to be the light of the world and a city on a hill. God has provided each of us with the precious gift of salvation through Jesus' sacrifice on the cross. It is our responsibility—no, our duty—to take the Good News of the Gospel to every corner of the earth so all can hear and decide (see Matthew 28:19–20).

Walk a different path. Take up your cross and bear the responsibility of showing love and grace to all whom you encounter.

#walkadifferentpath

Walk a different path.

See it there staring at you. It's there day and night and never goes away. You can't erase it, and you can't wipe it away or make it leave. Your reflection is who you are in the mirror, and it shows all of you—except what is in your heart.

God sees a reflection of you, too, only His image of you is not based upon your physical looks. God looks at the reflection of your heart and soul. He looks on the inside to measure what is truly important. God knows that the best of all of us comes from the strength and conviction of our relationship with Him, and that is what should be reflected on a hurting world.

Walk a different path. When you look in the mirror, take the Creator's view of your reflection (see 2 Corinthians 3:18).

#walkadifferentpath

Walk a different path.

All things come to an end, and this year is no different. We have seen the worst in people, experienced heartbreak and loss, and seen fear spread like a modern-day plague. Lines have been drawn, and the soul of our country has been taxed to its limits. We have forgotten the most basic of human qualities—common decency—in our drive to prove that we are right.

God saw this coming, for nothing takes Him by surprise. There is a way that seems right to man, but in the end it leads to destruction (see Proverbs 14:12; 16:25 NKJV). These words are in the Bible for a reason as God knows that we are prone to following our own understanding and not leaning on His. God wants to heal our hearts, which in turn will heal our relationships and our country, but we have to be willing to step aside and let Him do so. Only God can restore what we have lost. He promises that if we humble ourselves, seek His face, and turn from our wicked ways, He will hear from heaven, stretch forth His hand, freely forgive, and then heal our land (see 2 Chronicles 7:14).

Walk a different path. Let this year end by starting a relationship with the One who can heal and restore.

#walkadifferentpath

Part 2
WALKING THE PATH

Walk a different path.

It's painful to start. Like it is with anything new, there will be trepidation and concern. Beginnings are hard. Starting new and trying to make your way can be hard. Like starting a new year, which can be filled with promise, so can a new beginning, but we all seem to focus on the dread that surrounds that fresh start.

God is the God of new beginnings. One of my favorite statements from the Bible takes place shortly after the resurrection, when the angels are talking to the women who found the empty tomb. They want the women to tell Jesus' disciples—and Peter—that He will meet them (see Mark 16:7). Peter is mentioned specifically because I imagine Peter felt about an inch tall after denying Jesus three times before the crucifixion. But a new beginning awaited, and after Peter faced his failure, he became one of the most famous apostles.

Walk a different path. New beginnings can be uncertain, but God never is. Just ask Peter.

#walkadifferentpath

Walk a different path.

Many seek you, and few find you. We look in everyday life and hope we find you, but experience teaches us that you are not easy to grasp. To obtain you is like finding the greatest treasure of our lives, as you always lead us down the right path if we are blessed enough to find you. Wisdom, you are the ever-elusive gift for which we all strive.

Wisdom is a God-given trait for which we all should hope, and to be honest, ask for daily. Solomon was offered many things, but he chose to ask for wisdom. God honored his request and granted this to him, but because Solomon asked for wisdom, God gave him wisdom and so much more (see 2 Chronicles 1:7–12). God wants us to have wisdom in everything we do, and by that He means *godly* wisdom, so that we are not caught unawares of the traps of this life. The fear of the Lord is the beginning of wisdom (see Psalm 111:10; Proverbs 9:10); that doesn't mean God will destroy us or punish us, but that we must acknowledge His divinity and our need for Him. Asking for wisdom in all things should be what we strive for daily—even hourly—so we are able to discern what God truly wants for our lives.

Walk a different path. Rely on God's provision of wisdom, and the path will be clear on your journey.

#walkadifferentpath

Walk a different path.

Who among us can say they have been 100 percent faithful and loyal in every relationship they have had? Not that there was outright cheating, but being loyal to someone or something does not always mean not cheating on them. Oftentimes we can be disloyal when we feel we were betrayed or wronged in some way that truly is in our own minds.

God takes loyalty and faithfulness very seriously. The Word tells us that we are to remain ever faithful and that a friend loves at all times (see Proverbs 17:17). God wants us to look past this world, which promises us freedom and happiness, and see it is only through His strength and mercy that we can endure the pains in this life. By being loyal to His Word, we remain loyal to Him, the One who sticks closer than a brother (see Proverbs 18:24).

Walk a different path. Fear the Lord, the King, and do not join with those who do otherwise.

#walkadifferentpath

Walk a different path.

What does it mean to serve? Soldiers will volunteer, even give their lives in the name of their country as part of their service. We hold elections for representatives who are to serve the people in the halls of Congress, even though it often seems their service is to their own needs.

Service in God's eyes means serving Him and each other. We are called to serve Him through the way we live our lives, through the way we worship Him, and through the way we treat our fellow man. We serve each other by being there for one another and loving as He loves us. We are to bear one another's burdens (see Galatians 6:2; Romans 15:1) and continuously lift each other up in prayer. God loves it when we praise Him, but He also loves it when we treat each other according to His love for us.

Walk a different path. It is better to serve in heaven than it is to rule in hell.

#walkadifferentpath

Walk a different path.

Decisions face us every day. What will we wear? What will we eat? The decisions that seem to be getting made here lately in our country are of great concern. We have leaders who have their own agendas, who give no thought or care to their fellow man. Oh, they say they do, but actions speak louder than words.

God is not mocked. He is the sovereign Ruler over all creation, no matter who sits as president, vice president, speaker of the House, etc.—you get the point. There is not a decision we will make in our lives or as a people of which He is not already aware. God wants us to be wise in our decisions by lining them up according to His will. Why? Because He can see further down the road, and He is not surprised by all the chaos around us. He laughs at the evil around us because He knows its time is short (see Psalm 37:12–13).

Walk a different path. The One who rules in heaven laughs; the Lord scoffs at those who do evil.

#walkadifferentpath

Walk a different path.

Many things occupy our time: work, school, relationships, kids, other concerns. We are drawn to so many things, and so many checklist items occupy our time, and sometimes our—dare we say?—worship. A new car, a new job, a sports team we follow, or a favorite Hollywood actor. We fall down before the altars of the world and praise all that our human hands have made, even in the specialness of someone or something.

God will not share His glory. The Scripture says He is a jealous God (see Deuteronomy 4:24). God loves us, and He will not share us with the world. We belong to Him, and He proved that by sending His Son to die for us. No greater love than this exists, than that a man would lay down his life for his friends. Jesus did just that—so yes, I would say He has a right to be jealous when we put other things above His love. God has such an amazing plan for our lives, and it's because of His enduring love that we should worship Him for who He truly is: Friend, Father, and everlasting King.

Walk a different path. Save your worship for the One who has proven He deserves it.

#walkadifferentpath

Walk a different path.

We all have them. They can be good, and they can be bad, depending on how we are that day. Our feelings. Yes, our feelings—those ever-present sensations we experience every day of our lives. Fear, anger, rage—and even the positive ones like happiness and love. Feelings are part of who we are, and they can hurt or heal us at the same time.

God does not dwell in feelings, but in truth (see Deuteronomy 32:4). God does care about how we feel, but He also knows that our emotions need to be put in check from time to time. God does not do anything based on emotion, and truth be told, aren't we glad He doesn't? God wants us to dig deeper than emotions and feelings and seek the truth that is Him. The same truth that led Moses, made David a king, and welcomed Jesus into the world lies in all of us, and God wants to reveal that in each and every one of us—not through feelings, but in the knowledge that He is our Creator and He loves us.

Walk a different path. Don't search your feelings; search for He who is above those emotions.

#walkadifferentpath

Walk a different path.

We see the man hiding in the backseat on the movie screen. We scream at the couple to look in the back . . . he's in the back! . . . but unfortunately, this is a movie and they can't hear us. The movie may be fake—but fear is real, and sometimes it can cripple us. It doesn't have to be anything as terrifying as a slasher in the backseat. Fear of the unknown, of being alone, or of just about anything can bring us to our knees and cause us to cover up and curl in a ball, physically and emotionally.

God is not the author of fear. As a matter of fact, His Word says that perfect love drives out all fear (see 1 John 4:18). God has promised that He will ease our fears and comfort us in dark times if we will turn to Him and seek Him with all our hearts. The Creator of the universe is not afraid of the dark, nor is any fear too big for Him to overcome. Trust in His will for your life, and He will deliver you from the valley.

Walk a different path. When God is in the driver's seat, evil and fear can't stay in the back—they must jump out the window.

#walkadifferentpath

Walk a different path.

We never have enough of it. It seems like we rush and rush and wish we could save some in a bottle and use it later. We want it back when we lose someone, wish we could take something hurtful we said back, or stop our children from growing up. It is our most precious commodity—and it is time. Time is something that slips through our fingers so fast (see Psalm 31:15).

God is infinite, so time has no bearing on Him; however, He does understand our meaning of time. God asks that we use the time we are given to love one another, just as He has loved us. He asks that we serve one another, just as we serve Him. He asks that we have faith to know that when our time on earth comes to a close, because He loves us and died for us, we will experience infinite time with Him forever (see 1 John 2:17).

Walk a different path. The clock has no bearing on eternity—only our choices do.

#walkadifferentpath

Walk a different path.

Bear with me, because I am an "eighties kid" who loved Captain America and Optimus Prime. One fought for it, and the other said it was the right of every sentient being: Freedom. There are many speeches about it, and there are many songs extolling the virtues of freedom, but how many of us feel *truly* free? (see John 8:36). How many times have you looked at the world around you and saw that the freedom our forefathers fought and died for was being taken from you?

God sees all and knows all. Freedom is just as important to Him as it is to every single person on the planet. God does not lord Himself over us like some cruel dictator or a politician who thinks they know what is best for us. Rather, He is the ever-loving Father who speaks to our hearts and souls and offers a freedom in Him that can never be taken away. That freedom from sin was paid for at Calvary's cross, and Jesus is that doorway to the freedom we all crave and need.

Walk a different path. Freedom can never die if we go to the Life Source of all freedom.

#walkadifferentpath

Walk a different path.

What does it all mean? Is there a tabulation somewhere that shows the worth of a man or a woman? So many times, we have been told that we were not good enough or that we have messed up too badly, or worse yet, that we have been abandoned with no hope. What is our worth?

God believes that you are worth the price of His Son dying on a cross. God believes you are worth Him crossing through all time and space just to meet you where you are, right now, not later down the line. You don't have to get cleaned up to take a bath, and you don't need to believe you have no worth when God is on your side. The Word says that if God is for us, who can be against us? (see Romans 8:3). Trust in His promise that you are worth more than all the stars to Him.

Walk a different path. Remember, you are the apple of your Father's eye.

#walkadifferentpath

Walk a different path.

There is a feeling you can get, that makes it seem like you are suffocating. It arrives on the scene when you least expect it and turns your world upside down. Panic is no friend to anyone, and it can steal your breath, heart, and life away in an instant.

God does not ever panic, and He doesn't want us to, either. He is never taken by surprise because He knows the outcome of every situation. The words "do not be afraid" are spoken in the Bible exactly 365 times, and I like to think that it was put there to remind us not to fear every day of the year. Panic has no place in God's Kingdom and presence; therefore, it has no place in yours (see Isaiah 41:10).

Walk a different path. Do not be afraid; instead send panic packing.

#walkadifferentpath

Walk a different path.

Why is there so much going on in the world that is wrong? Why do our leaders make rules for us and then not follow those rules themselves? One word: *accountability*. We have lost the ability to be accountable for our actions, and we have glossed over the lawlessness and bad decisions we have made by calling it "social justice" or claiming that we were robbed of something.

God will hold us accountable for our actions individually, not as a group (Romans 14:10). He looks at each individual and examines their heart and decisions. God wants us to love, and He calls us to be accountable when we do something wrong, even if that means our cost will be great. When we are accountable for the things we say, think, and do, then God will be quick to forgive and honor our decision to repent and accept responsibility.

Walk a different path. Accountability is not hard, but it certainly is important.

#walkadifferentpath

Walk a different path.

Sometimes we lose something precious to us because of the choices we make. Truthfully, it might be restored, or sadly, it could be lost forever. Trust is the key in any relationship we have, whether it be with our spouse, our children, our family members, or even our friends and coworkers. Trust is the bridge that connects us all to one another, but many times we light the match to burn that bridge to the ground with no way to rebuild it.

God is all about trust. The phrase "trust in God" is mentioned 158 times in the Bible—and for good reason. God can rebuild any bridge we feel has been burned down, as long as we trust in Him to lead us to true repentance and forgiveness. Breaking trust, or having your trust broken, is not easy, but the Creator specializes in repairing that which is broken (see Proverbs 3:5).

Walk a different path. When you put your faith in God, construction of the bridge of trust can begin in any relationship.

#walkadifferentpath

Walk a different path.

There is a stalker that doesn't care who you are, what walk of life you are from, or how much you do or don't have. Pain does not play favorites. It will rip your heart in two and bring you to your knees. Mental pain, physical pain, emotional pain—it makes no difference, as pain has no remorse for the damage it inflicts.

God is very well acquainted with pain. From the emotional scene in the Garden of Gethsemane, to Judas's betrayal, to the torture of His Son and ultimately, His death on the cross of Calvary, our Father is well-versed in pain. That is why He can meet us in those dark places, where it seems the pain will not let us go. Jesus said to come to Him, all who are burdened (see Matthew 11:28)—many times we think that simply means "troubled," but He is also saying to come to Him with our pain. When we lay it down at the foot of the cross and walk away, God heals the body, soul, and heart.

Walk a different path. Pain is inevitable, but the cure is just a prayer away.

#walkadifferentpath

Walk a different path.

Heartache comes calling when we least expect it. Disaster is waiting around every corner and in every dark alley. Loss can happen in a moment's notice and leave us shaken to the core, or even shaking our fists toward heaven. Life certainly does not care what it throws at you, as long as it knocks you down. It may seem like there is nothing that can stop all the hurt in our lives.

Thankfully, we have a God who offers that one thing that *is* able to overcome—hope. Hope is that calming voice to the heartache that holds us in her arms. Hope sees the sun that rises after the disaster. Hope helps us with the loss we experience because she reminds us that there is another life where what we lost may yet be found again. God gives us hope by being the Father we need at the very time when we need it. Hope's sisters, Faith and Love, are always around, but Hope is the one that instills in us the idea that life can still be better.

Walk a different path. Hope will carry us to Faith, which will then carry us to Love (see Psalm 42:5).

#walkadifferentpath

Walk a different path.

In our world today, there is something off. Everyone is out for themselves or trying to get what is theirs, or what they think is theirs. We step on anyone who gets in our way, or we trample on anyone who doesn't think or believe the way we do. We lash out angrily, or sometimes violently, at anyone who gets in our way or doesn't hear "our truth."

God is absolute Truth. He knows what is right and what is wrong, and His thinking and ways are far beyond ours (see Isaiah 55:9). The Bible even states that no one can measure the depths of His understanding. God does not want us seeking the temporary, what we will get, who we will get, or how much; rather, He is more concerned about the condition of our hearts. Are we showing honor and following Him, or are we chasing something that, when we get it, it doesn't satisfy?

Walk a different path. Honor God and seek His truth. Everything else is just noise.

#walkadifferentpath

Walk a different path.

Watch as the birds fly through the sky, not a care in the world other than to soar in the sea of blue. Watch the waves as they crash on the beach, retreating back into the ocean only to roar back to the sand once again. Watch the sun as it rises and warms the earth and slowly crosses the sky until it sets in the evening, its work done for the day. Watch the moon and the light it gives the world, along with the hope of a good night's sleep.

God is the God of wonder. He created the birds and feeds them and cares for them, as they are His creatures (see Matthew 6:26). God told the oceans to come onto the sand only so far, and to roar as they do, providing the sweet sound that calms us when we are on the beach. God uses the sun to illuminate our day and to cause our fields to grow. He created the moon to bring us the coolness of night and to allow us to reflect. God created everything for His purpose, but none more important than you. As He told Moses, "Come, and I will show you My wonders." You are His most wonderful creation and truly a marvel to behold—always hold on to that.

Walk a different path. Wonder at His goodness and mercy, which He grants us every day (see Psalm 23:6).

#walkadifferentpath

Walk a different path.

What happens when we can't see beyond what is in front of us? When we look at situations and think, *Oh, that is a bad person*, or *That was a bad choice*? When we look at things with eyes of hatred or misunderstanding and cannot seem to grasp what the real issue is? We have been fooled by a world that does not want us to see the truth about what is really happening.

God is not fooled by anything. He sees all and knows all. Paul wrote in Ephesians that we war not against flesh (see Ephesians 6:12), but it seems we have forgotten this in the way we talk to and treat other people. God wants us to be as wise as serpents and as harmless as doves (see Matthew 10:16). We need to start seeing the real picture—the true battle He has been trying to show us. The spirits behind the hate and the bad things in the world do not come from a loving Creator.

Walk a different path. We know how the story ends, but let's be ever vigilant on the road to get there.

#walkadifferentpath

Walk a different path.

One of my all-time favorite movies is *Man on Fire* starring Denzel Washington. In the movie, he plays a man who hires himself out to be a bodyguard to a family in Mexico. He is distraught over his past and even tries to shoot himself, but the gun misfires. The character takes this as a sign and goes on to become quite close to the little girl he is hired to protect. When she is kidnapped and presumed dead, he proceeds to hunt down those responsible. Upon learning she is alive, he sacrifices himself in a trade so that she can live.

God knows what it's like to search for those who are lost (see Luke 19:10). He never gives up pursuing us, and just like the character in the movie, He made the ultimate sacrifice—His Son—on our behalf so that we might live. He experienced death and hell to save us because He doesn't want to live apart from us. He will calm storms, heal hearts, and save souls because His love for us is immeasurable.

Walk a different path. Remember there is a "God on Fire"—on fire with love for His children.

#walkadifferentpath

Walk a different path.

"What if?" is one of the worst feelings in the world. We wonder, *Maybe if I had only done this, or if I had just said that . . . What if I had been there sooner or made that phone call just a few minutes before?* *"What if?"* is the precursor to a life of regret, and it can swallow us up in indecision if we allow it to.

Everyone knows God did not give us a spirit of fear (see 2 Timothy 1:7), but He also does not want us to live in the past or with regrets. Ecclesiastes tells us that God keeps us so busy enjoying life that we take no time to brood over the past (see Ecclesiastes 5:18–20). God knows that today is enough; He wants us to live in the present and not be consumed by things from the past.

Walk a different path. Let go of yesterday and pursue your today filled with God's purpose.

#walkadifferentpath

Walk a different path.

Reality can set in real quick. A sudden loss of a loved one, the loss of a job, an accident, or a sick child or parent. Reality is a train that will keep on rolling, regardless of what is on the tracks. Reality does not concern itself with our problems or concerns, and it will shake us to our very core when we least expect it.

But reality holds no sway over God because He is above reality. God is not shocked or surprised by the reality train that rolls by in our lives. God asks us to place our trust in Him, not in the things of this world. When we do that, reality cannot hold sway over us, either, because we know He is with us and will not forsake us (see Hebrews 13:5).

Walk a different path. Make God your reality, and the train will roll smoother.

#walkadifferentpath

Walk a different path.

"Sorry, but the position has been filled." "I just want to be friends." "You weren't good enough to make the team, better luck next year." How many of us have heard these words—or at least some variation of them? Rejection is probably one of the worst feelings that we can experience.

Jesus knows exactly how we feel. As He was on the cross, He cried out, "My God, My God, why have You forsaken Me?" (see Matthew 27:46). For a brief moment, He was separated from the Father, rejected because of the sin He took upon Himself. Because of this moment in time, we can totally trust that He knows how we feel when we are rejected in life. He will never reject us because of His love for us, as evidenced by being rejected Himself to save us.

Walk a different path. God will not reject you, so reject the notion that you are not wanted or good enough.

#walkadifferentpath

Walk a different path.

As I sit here this morning, I'm looking at my daughter watching a video on the iPad. She is so focused on the movements of a little puppy, and she smiles as the image comes onto the screen. As I watch her, I think about how sweet and innocent she is and the lengths I would go to make sure she is safe and secure. She is my little girl, and as her daddy, it is my job to protect her and to reassure her that good always wins in the end.

God views us much like I view my daughter. When He looks at you and me, He sees His child, and He is immediately filled with love for us. God is so in love with us that He commands silence when even the weakest of us reaches out and accepts His gift of salvation. All of heaven rejoices when one of us makes that choice (see Luke 15:7). Let that sink in! The very Creator of all the wonderful things we see, rejoices the most when He is just talking with us. What an amazing love and an incredible Father!

Walk a different path. Remember to whom you belong and rest comfortably in His hands.

#walkadifferentpath

Walk a different path.

A few weeks ago, we went to Port Aransas on vacation. When I stepped onto the balcony from our room, I could hear the waves crashing on the beach. When we took the kids down to play, I watched as the waves came in, creeping closer and closer, eroded the beach and taking the sand back to the ocean. As I sit here this morning, those scenes remind me of how life can erode away at our hearts, how the waves can crash against our spirits, seemingly taking all the joy and hope out of our lives.

God is bigger than the ocean waves because He created the ocean and told the waves they could only come thus far (see Job 38:11). In the same manner, He orders the steps of our lives (see Psalm 37:23) and tells the waves that crash into us, "You can only come this far." Our Father loves us and will be with us through any storms that come against our lives. He is our strong tower and a mighty refuge, and He is faithful and willing to save us from the storms of life.

Walk a different path. Trust God and watch the waves recede.

#walkadifferentpath

Walk a different path.

It is getting darker later in the day, which is good because my kids can spend more time outside. It's funny how when they go to bed, it's still a little bit light outside, and they question, "Daddy, it's not dark. Why are we going to bed?" Innocent questions because they want to stay up and not surrender to the darkness—neither outside nor when they close their eyes. They fight for that one last moment to stay awake, to live every minute to the fullest.

God wants us to live our lives the same way my kids see it. To live every moment with Him and enjoy what He has blessed us with: our kids, our partner, girlfriend, boyfriend, or spouse. God has put a path in front of us, and He wants us to spend quality time with those we love and not regret any moments. We honor Him when we show that love and share it with those He has put in our lives.

Walk a different path. Darkness may come, but dance in the light as long as you can (see Ecclesiastes 5:18).

#walkadifferentpath

Walk a different path.

She is worth more than gold, and she is more precious than silver (see Proverbs 16:16). She can play hard to get, but to the person who catches her, she will prosper their lives forever. If only we would all pursue her diligently, perhaps we would not see our world in the state it is in now. Wisdom is a beautiful gift in that if we allow it to work in our lives, we would see such an amazing change in our world.

God treasures wisdom. He states that whoever lacks wisdom should simply ask (see James 1:5–6). Even King Solomon asked for wisdom above all else to rule his kingdom. God answered his prayer and made him the wisest man ever, and Solomon was blessed all his days. God wants us to walk in His wisdom every day because when we think like Him, we will never be led astray. His Spirit will guide us in all that we do—we only have to ask.

Walk a different path. Seek wisdom while she may be found and lean on God's understanding.

#walkadifferentpath

Walk a different path.

As I sit in my living room and look outside, the skies are cloudy, and it looks like rain. Sometimes clouds of fog envelop our lives and make it hard to see the sunshine. We walk around in the clouds, stumbling and feeling our way, all the while getting further and further lost within, until hope seems to fade away and we resign ourselves to the cloudiness that now seems to be our life.

God knows what these clouds are like. Calvary's cross was a cloudy day, and even Jesus felt alone. In these moments God shines the brightest. Jesus knew His death was necessary, but He also knew the Son would shine again. Three days after His death, the clouds parted, and the Son shone brighter than any day in history. God has shown us the way out of the clouds and leads us to walk with Him in the light (see 1 John 1:7).

Walk a different path. The Son lights the way, so step out of the clouds and walk with Him.

#walkadifferentpath

Walk a different path.

A child falls and scrapes her knee. An athlete grimaces when he injures his knee. Issues with physical pain are nothing new to us. "Something always hurts" is what we often say, especially as we get older. Physical pain can be hard, but we can always see the healing in our bodies as the pain subsides. But what about emotional or spiritual pain? The loss of a loved one, a failing marriage, or even the way we are talked to at times.

In his book *Where Is God When It Hurts?* Philip Yancey asked about the pain we feel in our lives and whether there is a God who truly cares. God cares—of that there is no doubt. The Creator of our universe cares for every hurt we experience in our lives. God knows our physical pain is temporary, but He also knows that spiritual and emotional pain need His touch to heal completely. He heals the brokenhearted, binds up their wounds, and saves those who are crushed in spirit (see Psalm 147:3; 34:18). God has promised to wipe every tear from our eyes and hold us close to Him for eternity. Our present sufferings are nothing compared to this promise (Romans 8:18).

Walk a different path. Pain hurts in all forms, but God is the Healer and the Restorer of our souls.

#walkadifferentpath

Walk a different path.

The other day I lost the magnet that holds my phone to my dashboard when I am in the car. It's the second one I have lost, so I went to the store and bought another. I found the one I lost stuck to my washer yesterday. Somehow the magnet stuck, and I didn't see it, so I just laughed because I never checked the laundry room when I lost it. Funny how something so trivial made me laugh so hard.

Imagine a Creator who sees a son or daughter who was lost come back to Him. The famous parable of the prodigal son shows how God runs to us when we come home (see Luke 15:11–24). The most beautiful thing that happens is God's call for silence in heaven when someone calls upon His name. All of heaven then rejoices when that person accepts His gift of salvation. Just imagine that: all of heaven rejoiced when you came to the Father!

Walk a different path. God gave everything to be with us. Imagine the party He will throw when we arrive home.

#walkadifferentpath

Walk a different path.

My oldest son loves storms—as long as they are in a movie or in a book. He is fascinated by how they work and what causes them. To be honest, he is pretty much into any natural disaster. He is always asking me about tornadoes, hurricanes, tsunamis, etc. His fascination with these weather patterns and how much he studies them in videos or books amazes me. It's all awesome to him—until an actual storm blows in. Then, I can hear the fear in his voice and see it in the way he shakes. He is okay as long as the storm isn't real in his world.

Jesus slept in the boat, but He awoke when the disciples called out to Him for help. "Peace, be still," He said to the storm, and all was calm. Pay attention to that command. Jesus basically told the storm to shut up and calm down. While He would never tell us to just "shut up," He does speak to our hearts and reminds us that He is in control and we should be calm. If He calmed the storm and waters then, how much more will He now that He lives in each of us? He has promised to be with us, even to the end, and He is faithful to His Word (see Matthew 28:20).

Walk a different path. Storms may come, but "peace, be still" will still reign.

#walkadifferentpath

Walk a different path.

She can blindside you. Make you say and do things you didn't think possible. Love is that wonderful feeling we all long for. It's the smile from a spouse, the touch of the hand by a girlfriend, the laugh of your child. Love has many faces and many emotions tied to it.

God is the ultimate Giver of love (see John 3:16). He gave His Son for each of us as a pure demonstration of His love. And as if that wasn't enough, He still shows us love by being there for us when we are heartbroken, feel alone, or are just in need of someone to care. God crossed the universe just to meet us where we are, and He did it because of His great love for us.

Walk a different path. Love is eternal and can overcome anything—just look at Calvary's cross.

#walkadifferentpath

Walk a different path.

By definition, *honor* is a matter of carrying out and living the values of respect, duty, loyalty, selfless service, integrity, and personal courage in everything you do. It's giving your word and standing by that word. It's doing what is right, no matter the cost. In a world where honor seems to have slipped away, we see the effects that is having on our country, our relationships, and our lives.

God respects and admires the honor we show Him, as well as the honor we show others. God tells us to honor our mothers and fathers. God tells us to honor our word and to always focus on what is good and true. The psalmist said it best: *"But giving thanks is a sacrifice that truly honors me. If you keep to my path, I will reveal to you the salvation of God"* (Psalm 50:23 NLT). By showing honor to God in all we do, He will show us wonders we have never seen before. He has already showed the greatest wonder in that He died for us.

Walk a different path. Honor is not lost in the world when we have a God who can show us how to restore it.

#walkadifferentpath

Walk a different path.

Everyone wants to fit in or belong. What is the old saying? We all want to be loved. Everyone wants to feel accepted, to know they matter. No one wants to feel alone or useless, yet that is how the world treats some of us. It grinds us up and spits us out with no thought to how we feel. A sense of belonging and acceptance is the longing of every heart, and love is the goal of every soul.

With God, you don't have to wonder whether you are accepted or belong, and you certainly do not have to wonder whether or not you are loved. You are enough because He created you and His love for you knows no limits. "I knew you before I formed you in your mother's womb," God tells us (Jeremiah 1:5 NLT). You are accepted, you belong, and you are wanted and loved because you are a child of the King.

Walk a different path. Eternity with God awaits; this world is just a stepping-stone to get there.

#walkadifferentpath

Walk a different path.

Our moods change constantly. Sometimes we are so happy that it seems we can open our arms and fly to the sky. Nothing can bring us down, and we soar through the clouds without a care in the world. Then there are those other times. Times when we feel so low, that same sky seems to crush us beneath its weight. We feel like the whole world is on our shoulders, and we don't know when or if we will ever feel alive again.

God does not change in His moods—and thank goodness for that! We do not serve a God of moods or emotions, but an everlasting Father who only wants what is best for us. He has promised He will soar with us when we are flying high in the sky, but more importantly, He has promised to carry us when we are at our lowest. He does not change—He is "the same yesterday, today, and forever" (Hebrews 13:8 NLT)—and because He is, we know He will always have us in His hands.

Walk a different path. Moods may swing, but God is always constant.

#walkadifferentpath

Walk a different path.

We have all seen a lake on a beautiful morning and the stillness that it brings. Or maybe we have heard the gentle sounds of a river as its waters move or heard the ocean waves silently crest on the shore. But what happens when that lake has rough, choppy waters, or that river rises in floodwaters, or that ocean roars and sends waves violently crashing past the shoreline? All these things can happen to us in our daily lives. Our lives are no longer calm—rough waters lie ahead, and we feel like we are drowning with no escape.

"Peace, be still!" Jesus said this as the waves were crashing and the disciples were terrified (Mark 4:39 NKJV). Jesus restored the calm on the seas, and He can do the same for us when the waters in our lives are raging. He promised He would never leave us or forsake us (see Hebrews 13:5), that He would be with us, even unto the end (see Matthew 28:20). That is a promise we can believe because He has shown us He is faithful, even when we are not. He will restore our souls as His Word says, as He makes us to lie down in green pastures (see Psalm 23). The God of the universe is more than a match for any storm that comes our way, no matter how raging it is.

Walk a different path. The calm in our lives may be threatened, but God can restore it to our hearts, no matter how loud the storm.

#walkadifferentpath

Walk a different path.

We are all being chased by something. Sometimes it's a dog, sometimes it's the police (I hope not!), and sometimes it's our past. In true honesty, we are all being chased by death. A dog can be subdued, you can pull over and surrender to the cops, and it is possible to let go of the past, but mortality is something that weighs on everyone's mind and heart, even if we don't care to admit it. Fear rises in all of us when we lose a loved one, and we remember that chase is in our lives, too. *What is next?* we wonder.

God has made no secret about the next stage in our lives. "It is appointed for men to die once" (Hebrews 9:27 NKJV). This can sound really scary, but God wants us to have hope. In life, we go on journeys, and we walk through doors. Eternity cannot be reached without casting off our human form, so death is a necessary door through which we must walk. And oh, what awaits us on the other side! A loving Father who has promised to wipe every tear from our eyes (see Revelation 7:17; 21:4). Let that sink in! The God of the universe loves you so much that He can't wait to wipe away your every tear.

Walk a different path. The chase doesn't need to scare us because God rules over all. And please just pull over if a cop is behind you!

#walkadifferentpath

Walk a different path.

I am a diehard Rangers fan. I love baseball, and that is my team. I was so excited when they went to the World Series in 2011 because, I finally thought, *This is the year! Finally they will do it!* Then game six happened, bringing shattered expectations and broken dreams. Yes, it was just a baseball game, but it still broke my heart. How much more are our hearts broken when our dreams are crushed and our spirits feel at their lowest? We work hard at something and we pray, but it all falls apart before our eyes like some slow-motion horror movie.

God is the Comforter of shattered dreams. He wants the absolute best for us, and He longs to give our lives true fulfillment. When we trust in Him, we can honestly look at situations where we think our dreams are shattered and realize that He has something better for us. His Word says that He knows the plans He has for us (see Jeremiah 29:11). If God can create the universe and every living thing in it, He can also be trusted to know what is best for us.

Walk a different path. Trust God with your hopes and dreams because He cares about them—even my favorite baseball team.

#walkadifferentpath

Walk a different path.

I have never seen war up close. I have seen it on television and in movies, where Hollywood dresses it up and tries to imitate life, but to me, something seems missing in those depictions. Friends and family members of mine have served, and I am told that the very act will change you. Truthfully, I have seen this in some of those family members and friends. War can change you physically, mentally, and emotionally. But what about the spiritual war going on all around us? The fight we don't see with our natural eyes?

Paul tells us that we war not against flesh, but the spirits in the dark places (see Ephesians 6:12). How do we fight an enemy unseen? How can we protect those we love? Once again, Paul tells us to put on the whole armor of God so we can withstand the enemy (verses 13–18). And the sword we fight with is the Word of God (verse 17). We can know that sword will never break because it's His Word and He never breaks His Word. He promised to equip us, and He has, but we have to accept the armor and steadfastly pray against those spirits.

Walk a different path. Put on your armor, and report for duty.

#walkadifferentpath

Walk a different path.

I sleep with a fan on at night. It may seem noisy to others, but I find a certain peace and stillness in it. *Stillness.* What a word in our spoken language. For some it means watching a baby sleep, or that good night's rest we have been needing. There is so much noise and commotion going on in the world that I believe we all would like a little stillness in our lives, our hearts, and our souls.

God has a plan for our stillness. His Word says, "Be still and know that I am God" (Psalm 46:10 NKJV). What an amazing statement! The Creator of all things sees our hurt, our pain, our fears, and all that pertains to us, and He says, "Be still and know." God says this because He knows everything that will happen, has happened, and is happening. He is never caught off guard. It is through this stillness that we can hear His voice that guides us.

Walk a different path. Be still and know that He is God. Then not even the fan will be noisy in the stillness.

#walkadifferentpath

Walk a different path.

How many times have I sat here and listened to the sounds all around me? I have flown in airplanes, including over the Grand Canyon, looked down, and thought, *Wow, that is amazing.* What amazes me even more is that I am traveling over five hundred miles an hour, supported by wings that probably weigh less than the body of the plane. I have also looked at the fury of thunderstorms, been amazed at the beauty of a flower blooming, and marveled at the birth of my children.

Wonder. God's wonder. He shows us His wonders every day if we will just take the time to recognize them. A hug from your child, a gentle touch from a mate, the wisdom from our elders. These are all part of God's wonders, which He shows us daily, but the Bible tells us that "no eye has seen, no ear has heard, and no mind has imagined what God has prepared for those who love him" (1 Corinthians 2:9 NLT). I am speechless when I think about this, and I'm blown away at how much He loves us.

Walk a different path. Take time to behold the wonders you can see around you because the best is yet to come.

#walkadifferentpath

Walk a different path.

There is no worse of a dream killer than doubt, especially the self-doubting kind. Like a poison, self-doubt seeps into your heart and causes fear; it can paralyze us spiritually, emotionally, and sometimes even physically. It is constantly seeking anyone who will accept it and allow it to take root in their lives. Doubt does not care about how much money you have, where you live, where you work, or what kind of car you drive. Doubt welcomes all who will let it in.

God does not dwell in the realm of doubt. Many times, He has told us to have faith and believe. Faith and belief are God's mighty tools against doubt. He wages that war for us, reminding us of His great love and that through Him, we all have a future and a hope (see Jeremiah 29:11), free from the curse of doubt. God says, "My child, I have you—and that is enough."

Walk a different path. Although doubt can creep in, God can sweep it out.

#walkadifferentpath

Part 3
THE JOURNEY CONTINUES

Walk a different path.

I close my eyes and soak it in. The beats, the words, the simplicity that the music brings. My heart leaps with every rise in the chorus, to the bridge line that reinforces the words. It's not just music; it's not just words. *Worship.* There is nothing quite like it, nothing more freeing. Even as I type these words, I feel the worship rising within me.

Everything under the heavens and on the earth was created to praise our Creator (see Psalm 150:6). God desires our worship, and why should He not get it? He has given us the breath of life and made a path for us to come home. He delights in our worship and our adoration of Him. It is our moment to draw near to Him, just as He draws near to us (see James 4:8).

Walk a different path. Worship with all your heart and let our Father speak to your soul.

#walkadifferentpath

Walk a different path.

I remember how I felt looking at it. That new toy that was advertised on television, so shiny as it called to me. I wanted it. I remember when I first saw that girl when I was younger, and I wanted to be her boyfriend more than anything. I wanted to be with her. I remember when I saw them in their caskets, my soul screaming, *Come back!* I wanted them to live. We all have wants. Yes, there is a difference between a want and a need. I want to be a good dad. I want to have her look at me and want me, and me alone. I want my family and friends to be safe. I want.

God is not a strict disciplinarian who slaps our hands when we want something. Rather, He is such a loving Father, and yes, He will supply our needs—but He also desires to give us what we want, to the extent that it does not endanger us. See, He knows what the road looks like ahead of us, so He give us the wants and needs that line up with His will (see Matthew 6:33).

Walk a different path. It's okay to want things, but focus your number-one want on knowing your Father in heaven and doing His will.

#walkadifferentpath

Walk a different path.

I didn't see when the curves of life would come, the bumps that would strand me on life's highway, alone and lost. I remembered all this last week while thinking of a song called "I Still Believe." Its words—"Even when I don't see, I still believe"—have been on my heart and in my mind, haunting my thoughts and prayers. What is God trying to tell me?

God knows that life will be bumpy, but we are never alone on the road of life because He pilots and directs us through the rough times (see Proverbs 3:5–6). He also places thoughts, words, or songs in our hearts and minds to remind us of His love and His hand on our lives. God answered that for me in church today as the message was about believing even when we can't see. God placed that special message there for me because He knew that's what I needed, and He does that for all of us.

Walk a different path. Allow God to speak to you and then wait patiently. Even when you can't see, you can believe He is God and is able.

#walkadifferentpath

Walk a different path.

Fog is prevalent in many places. Driving over the Bay Bridge in San Francisco in the morning in the fall, or as it rolls in on the East Coast, the fog can make it hard to see and cause real havoc if we aren't careful. But what about the fog that encompasses our hearts and blinds us to everything around us? When it is so thick, you feel you may choke on it, you can't breathe, and you just curl up in a ball because you can't find your way out?

God is so amazing that He can see through the fog, on the bridge, at the coast, and especially in our hearts and minds. God is the Light that shines in the darkness (see John 8:12), because as the song says, "He is the Way Maker." God takes us by the hand and leads us down the paths of righteousness, for His name's sake. He will clear the fog from our hearts and open our eyes so we see clearly, and then, in turn, see Him for who He truly is: a loving Father who would send His own Son to the cross for His children.

Walk a different path. God is our Lighthouse; allow Him to shine and the fog will roll away.

#walkadifferentpath

Walk a different path.

I have read many stories and seen many movies where a ship just disappears. Lost at sea, with no trace. Or person leaves their house and is never seen again. Lost in humanity. Even my kids will misplace something, and then it's gone. Lost in our residence. But what about that feeling that your heart and soul have checked out, when you feel lost inside and you can't explain why? The feeling that you are wading in deep waters, and you are overwhelmed and weighed down by the feeling of being lost and alone.

Jesus felt that way on the cross. When He was about to die, He cried out the saddest words ever spoken: "My God, My God, why have You forsaken Me?" (Matthew 27:46 NKJV). Those words echoed off the cross and the hill at Calvary with a sadness that even now can be felt if we allow ourselves to live in that moment. But because He uttered those words, we can now reach out to our Creator and ask why He has forsaken us. The wonderful part is that He will answer, "I never left, just as I was there for My Son." See, God allowed Jesus to take our place, and when all our reasons for being lost were poured out on Him, He said, "It is finished." Jesus became the ship that was found, the person who turned up, and He bridged the gap of those deep waters and lifted the weight off us.

Walk a different path. It's okay to feel lost; just know that God is the Compass of your soul, and He knows the way home.

#walkadifferentpath

Walk a different path.

Dreams get shattered, hearts get broken, and feelings seem to spiral out of control. Sometimes it's hard to see the ray of light shining through the dark clouds of our lives. We have so many things that seem to knock us down or slam into us, like waves crashing in the ocean. We want to just curl up in a ball and say, "No more, I am done. What is the point, and why should I care?"

Perseverance is God's answer to these questions. He never promised it would be easy to walk in this world; as a matter of fact, Jesus said we *would* have trouble, but He has overcome the world (see John 16:33). Perseverance in all we do is key to a life in Him, for He stated, "To him who overcomes I will give the crown of life." God will never leave you. He will be that voice that tells you to get up one more time and try again. Why? Because He created you, He knows your worth, and He gives you His strength.

Walk a different path. Persevere in this life, because rest is up ahead with Him.

#walkadifferentpath

Walk a different path

Failure is so debilitating. It reaches into your soul, turning you inside out. It doesn't care who sees. It twists and turns within you and makes you want to shrink back and hide in a hole. Whether it be at the job or at home, failure is not like its cousin, pride, as failure does not care who you are or where you come from. Failure seeks to destroy your relationships, your mood, and even your spiritual walk.

God has an answer to failure. It is called grace (see Ephesians 2:8–9). Grace will reach in and turn our lives back to the One who can take our failure and show us the meaning of that grace. No matter the failure, God is there offering grace to show that we can try again, that we can go that extra mile, and that it isn't over when we stumble. God whispers, "Try again, My child," as His grace pours over our hearts and souls.

Walk a different path. Failure can trip you, but grace picks you up to try again.

#walkadifferentpath

Walk a different path.

Everyone has stood outside and felt the wind on their face or has seen the leaves blowing through the trees. The wind is invisible, yet we can see the effects the wind has. Sometimes our lives can feel like the wind, in that we feel invisible. We believe no one sees us, or worse, that no one cares to see us. The feeling of loneliness that creeps in when we feel invisible, especially to those who say they love us, can grip our hearts and crush our spirits.

God is invisible to our eyes, but His glory and love are not. We can see the love our Creator has for us by observing His majesty in the clouds, the amazing ingenuity in how a plane works, or the magical moment a baby is born. God wants you to know that you are not invisible to Him and that He loves you very much, so much so that His Son died for you. Invisible to the eyes He may be for now, but imagine the happiness we will feel when we actually see Him face-to-face (see 1 Corinthians 13:12).

Walk a different path. You are not invisible, and God is ever present.

#walkadifferentpath

Walk a different path.

Fear is a difficult thing to deal with. It comes in all shapes and sizes, from the fear of heights, to the fear of insects, the fear of losing someone you love, and quite possibly most people's greatest fear, the fear of death. Fear can grip us and cut off our spiritual, emotional, and sometimes physical selves from reality, causing us to go into "instant panic" mode or freeze in place, with no strength or will to break free. Fear can grip the very soul of a person and hold them hostage within themselves, refusing to budge an inch.

Fear is not of God. That bears repeating: Fear is not of God. The words "fear not" are found in the Bible 365 times, or, as I like to look at it, once for each day of the year. God does not give us a spirit of fear (see 2 Timothy 1:7), and He does not want us to spend one minute living our lives in fear. He has promised He will always be with us and walk with us, even in the darkest valleys. God is Light, and fear cannot stand in the light.

Walk a different path. Remember never to fear this life because God holds you safely in His hands.

#walkadifferentpath

Walk a different path.

Today has been very busy. With so many calls at work and the daily grind of a career—my, where has the time gone? It seems we step outside the comfort of our beds, feet already churning to start the day, and then it starts. Life. The everyday nature of what we do, our responsibilities, the people we love and take care of—it all comes to a head very quickly, from that first step. Life roars on like a freight train, and it can run you down just as fast.

God understands that we have things we need to do, but He wants us to realize that nothing is more important than seeking Him (see Jeremiah 29:13; Proverbs 8:17). "Be still and know that I am God," He calls to us, not to show off His impressive power and authority, but to give us a new perspective (see Psalm 46:10). He wants to shield us from the everyday rush as we seek that which is important, a relationship with Him.

Walk a different path. No human phone call can ever replace the call God has on your life.

#walkadifferentpath

Walk a different path.

Many things in this world can hurt. Breaking a bone, accidentally cutting yourself with a knife, and being in an accident rank right up there. But there is something else that is right up there in the realm of hurt—and that is betrayal. Have you been betrayed by a friend who said they would always have your back, been betrayed by a significant other whose eyes and emotions wandered, or even felt betrayed by your children when they moved away or started coming around or involving you less in their lives? Betrayal is ugly, cutting not just to the heart, but to the very soul of an individual. It starts the domino effect of the loss of trust and hope, and in many cases, the ability to love and forgive.

Jesus is well acquainted with betrayal. One of His friends sold Him out for thirty pieces of silver, and when the going got rough in the garden, His friends took off and left Him alone, and one of His closest friends even denied knowing Him, not once, but three times. Yes, our Savior is well-versed in betrayal, and He knows how you feel when this happens to you. We must always look to His example, to His very own words: "Father, forgive them, for they do not know what they do" (Luke 23:34 NKJV). The key word here is "forgive"—and that's what He wants from us, to walk in His forgiveness regardless of the circumstance.

Walk a different path. Betrayal is nasty, and it hurts, but nail-scarred hands hold you up and prepare your heart to forgive.

#walkadifferentpath

Walk a different path.

Hallmark movies, especially the Christmas ones, are pretty easy to figure out. The plot involves a man and a woman, usually at opposite ends, who fall in love with each other as romance blossoms. Romance. I know I am not a writer, and I don't a novel to my name, yet even I do like romance in my life. To feel needed and wanted by someone, someone who genuinely likes, cares, and loves you, is one of the best feelings in the world. Romance can make us do things and say things that are out of our character, but all the same, we all want to feel that emotion, and dare I say, be swept off our feet by it.

There is no greater example of romance than the love story God has for each and every one of us: For God so loved us that He gave us His only Son as a ransom in our place (see John 3:16). Even when we were far away from Him, He pursued us as any lover would, going to any lengths to bring us safely back to His arms. The romance between God and His people has been spoken about, written about, and sung about for years, and because of this great pursuit and love, we can know there is truly a Person who cherishes us and wants nothing but the best for us. There cannot be any better example of romance that what our heavenly Father shows us.

Walk a different path. God's love is better than any movie, because His romance is not an act of fiction.

#walkadifferentpath

Walk a different path.

I will be forty-nine years old in May. My youngest son believes he is stronger than me because I am "old." He always is grabbing my arm and holding on to it, which, in turn, I start moving back and forth as he bounces like a rag doll. He is playing with me, but he still thinks he is stronger. Feats of strength are cool, but there are times when we don't feel so strong. The loss of a job, the loss of a loved one, or just a very bad month can cause us to feel weak, sometimes physically, but most times spiritually and emotionally. We feel we can't go on and that we should just stay where we are and not move.

Jesus knows all too well about failing strength—on all levels. In the Garden of Gethsemane, the Bible tells us, Jesus was in such despair, such weakness, that as He prayed, His sweat became as drops of blood (see Luke 22:44). Jesus knew what was coming, and His strength was fading, even to the point that He asked the Father if He could avoid what was coming. Jesus knows what it is like to lose strength, which is why He can meet you right where you are in whatever moment you find yourself. He tells us that we can come, anyone who is burdened, and He will give us rest. He restores our souls (see Psalm 23:3), and He intercedes to the Father on our behalf.

Walk a different path. Strength can come and go, but a risen, victorious Savior is always there to restore us.

#walkadifferentpath

Walk a different path.

We all have those days when everything comes crashing down. We can't breathe, can't speak. Just taking a step is agony, and words escape us. We pray and feel like we get no answer, that hope has abandoned us. Our very souls feel like they are dying, and no words of comfort seem to fit.

This is how Jesus must have felt on Good Friday. He had pleaded that the cup He faced could be taken from Him; all His friends had abandoned Him; He was beaten for no reason and then nailed to a cross for no crime. Even on the cross, He asked, "My God, why have You forsaken Me?" (see Mark 15:34). Good Friday had to happen—and Jesus knew it did—but that didn't change His feelings toward the process. That is why He can reach down into our hearts and souls today and comfort us when everything seems to be falling apart. Good Friday was the moment when Jesus said, "I love you so much that I am going to die for you."

Walk a different path. Good Friday is for all of us, giving us a front-row view of how much we are worth to and loved by our Savior.

#walkadifferentpath

Walk a different path.

Despair can creep in when you least expect it. Loss can cause it, or sometimes just feeling that you are alone will drive you to think you are always going to be that way and that nothing really matters. Despair is a crippling disease, but there is a cure for despair that sometimes we don't see. It is there all the time, staring us in the face, encouraging us to get up and try again, to know that life is hard but there is a new day waiting. That cure is hope.

God is the Author of hope (see Romans 5:5). Look anywhere in the Bible and you will see it. Abraham hoped for a child. Israel hoped for deliverance from Egypt. David hoped to be a man after God's own heart. Esther hoped to save her people. The stories of the hope God gives are so numerous, and they remind us of who really is in control of this life. God never said there wouldn't be dark times, but it is through the hope He provides that we can look to brighter days ahead.

Walk a different path. Despair loves the darkness, but God uses hope to illuminate the darkness and bring us into His light (see Romans 15:13).

#walkadifferentpath

Walk a different path.

I know am not the world's best person. I get angry and say things I don't mean, or I can shut down when people try to talk to me. As I sit here, I am reminded of when Renae died. I was upset and sad, but I also remember that a strange peace settled over me. Now I am not so calm and not so peaceful, as it seems heartbreak and loss keep following me. I have yelled at God, and I have not been what you would call "nice" as I grieve the loss of my wife.

God is very big, and He understands when we are in pain. He is not afraid, nor are His feelings hurt when we yell at Him, as I did today. God knows our pain is real, and He longs to draw us close (see James 4:8) and comfort us on our darkest days. He is a forgiving God because He knows that we can't see what's ahead, but rather He waits for us to reason with Him after He has calmed our souls so that healing can begin.

Walk a different path. God can handle it when we are upset, and He is always there to say, "Fear not, My child."

#walkadifferentpath

Walk a different path.

I am trying to teach my kids certain lessons in life. I have held a dollar in my hand and a quarter. Both have value, but as I explained to them, one is worth more. *Worth.* Such a powerful description of items, but even more so for people. How is a person's worth measured? Is it by the things they do, the wealth they accumulate, or what circles they run in? What happens when you feel like you are not worth anything, like you have been cast aside or disregarded?

God believes in your worth, so much so that He gave His only Son to die for *you*. Imagine that—that Someone would give up His most precious thing just to show you your value to Him, your worth. There has never been a love so greatly shown, and when we feel like we are worthless and not valued, He sweeps in and reminds us of Cavalry. He wants you to know that there is no length He wouldn't go to in order to show His love for you (see 1 John 3:1).

Walk a different path. Dollars and quarters can buy some things, but your true worth is as a child of our loving Father.

#walkadifferentpath

Walk a different path.

Struggle is common to every person. Some people may struggle in school, such as with math or reading. Others may struggle at work because they don't understand something or don't feel fulfilled in what they are doing. Still others struggle when they lose someone, whether through a breakup or death. Struggle is very real to the human condition; it can sometimes choke us and lead us down a path of misery from which it seems there is no escape. We may feel like we have fallen into a hole and are trying to claw our way out, but as the saying goes, "the struggle is real."

God never said we would have easy lives; in fact, He told us some struggles would come. He also told us not to worry because He would be with us—always. Jesus said, "Come to Me, all you who are burdened, and I will give you rest," and I believe that was for the times of struggle He knew we would encounter. Jesus does not look at us in disappointment because we struggle, but rather He encourages to take one more step, or forgive one more time. He is rooting for us with the promise that He will not burden us because He is gentle and His burden is light (see Matthew 11:29–30).

Walk a different path. Struggles will come, and they may seem impossible, but Jesus specializes in making the possible out of the impossible.

#walkadifferentpath

Walk a different path.

Choices are sometimes easy and sometimes hard. Where to live, where to work, who you are with or not, even how you raise your kids—it all involves a choice. Some choices are easy: taking a shower, brushing your teeth, and getting dressed every day are easy enough, but what about those choices that rip your heart out? You know the ones I am talking about. The ones you didn't make for yourself, like when a loved one passes away, or your heart gets broken, or your job shuts down and moves overseas. It's these choices of others that make us feel helpless and that no one understands, even if someone else has been through it. The choices that are made without our input can lead us to choose to be overcome with grief, to feel jaded and as if there is no place for us.

God gave us free will so that we could choose, but He longs for us to choose Him because He knows our steps. He is that voice in your heart and mind telling you to not go that way, not to accept that job or walk away from that friend. He does not want to choose for us, but He wants us to use His wisdom and understanding when it comes to making our life choices. No one can measure the depths of His understanding and love, and because of these traits, we can trust that He will help us make the right choice, every time (see Deuteronomy 30:19).

Walk a different path. Choose life so that you may live, and don't sweat the small stuff.

#walkadifferentpath

Walk a different path.

I have had a lot of loss in recent years. Losing Renae was probably the most gut-wrenching thing to happen to me in all my life. I lost my person, my best friend, and my wife all rolled up in one. My kids did not get to spend much time with their mom. I lost my own mom shortly thereafter, and I never got to say goodbye. My kids lost a grandmother in the process. I have since lost another family member, as well as other friends—enough to where I started to wonder what the plan was.

God never made it a secret that we cannot enter eternity how we are. It's not that He doesn't appreciate His creation, but it is a vessel of sin, and sin cannot enter heaven. Although it may seem there is no plan, Jesus said He was going to prepare a place for us (see John 14:2–3), and I believe every person who accepts Him gets put on the list for a new home. Renae and Mom had their names called because He had finished their homes and called them to come and live with Him for eternity.

Walk a different path. Jesus has never broken His Word yet; someday your house will be completed, and He will call your name.

#walkadifferentpath

Walk a different path.

This has happened to me once, and I know I am not the only one. The gas light in my vehicle came on, but I ignored it and eventually ran out of gas. Empty tank. Most of us have had the feeling of an empty tank—and I am not just talking about the car. Emptiness can come into our lives and make us feel hollow and cold inside. We feel detached from everything and everyone around us, due to losing someone—or let's just say it, from dealing with everyday life. The icy grip of emptiness grabs our hearts and takes us down a path of loneliness, bringing a sense of sadness that we sometimes don't even feel because we are just so empty.

God wants to fill the void of emptiness we feel in our hearts. He doesn't remove the void; He fills it. He fills the void with purpose—to live for the glory of God, who died for you. When we allow God to fill the emptiness inside, we allow Him to show us a better path and a more fruitful life, without the burden of feeling empty and alone. He has stated He will never leave us nor forsake us, and that we are His, no matter what (see Song of Solomon 6:3). His perfect love will fill any hole inside us and bring us to an everlasting peace with Him.

Walk a different path. You may run out of gas, but your life will never be empty because you never run out of God.

#walkadifferentpath

Walk a different path.

My oldest son struggles sometimes with conveying his feelings. He was very close to his mom, and there is some anger there from losing her, so much so that he lashes out. Now, that is no excuse, but he is going through what we all go through in life. Struggle. Struggle can come from anything really, whether at work, at school, or just in everyday life. We can feel weighed down emotionally and sometimes physically, and we lash out or retreat to a dark place in our hearts and minds so that we can forget the world and just try and catch a breath.

Jesus never said we wouldn't struggle; in fact, He said specifically that in this world there *would* be trouble. Jesus has never lied to us, and He wanted to let us know right from the start that we would see trouble. It is what He says after that that brings us hope: "But take heart; I have overcome the world" (John 16:33 ESV). Our Savior is showing us that we can overcome the struggles of life because the same Spirit that raised Him from the dead resides in us, and because He overcame, we can, as well.

Walk a different path. Struggles will come, but look to the One who has your back and helps you overcome.

#walkadifferentpath

Walk a different path.

I don't sleep well. I really haven't in many years. I just can't seem to turn off my mind at night and rest. *Rest.* Funny how that word can speak so loudly to us. We long for rest from the day, from situations, from stress and anxiety. We long for rest for our bodies, but if we are truly honest with ourselves, the real problem is that our souls are tired. We need rest from all the hurt, heartache, and pain that has happened to us, so much that it's affecting our physical body, as well. We long for rest for the soul in a world that has beaten us down.

Jesus said, "Come to Me all who are heavy burdened, and I will give you rest" (see Matthew 11:28). Jesus knew how tired our souls would become, and He offers us rest and peace if we will come to Him. It really is that simple: we just need to allow Him to take the burden and rest in Him, knowing that He loves us and longs to show us a better way to live, free from burdens. He wants us to comfortably rest in Him.

Walk a different path. Find rest in the arms of the One who can take your burdens away and give you the peace your soul longs for.

#walkadifferentpath

Walk a different path.

We all have them. Some are good, some are bad, some are indifferent. We have them every day, regardless of which way the door swings. We all have choices, and there is always a consequence or action that goes along with each choice we make. If you decide not to get up and go to work, then you will get fired. If you decide not to put gas in your car, then you will ultimately have to walk or even push your vehicle. But what about those choices that we didn't ask for? Like when a loved one who has lived a clean life gets cancer? Or when a child suffers from abuse? Or when a spouse betrays their significant other? Choices that we don't make ourselves are often the hardest to reconcile; they can even make us bitter and closed off to those around us.

God has given us free will—for love should be chosen, not forced—and He will hold us accountable for our choices. However, many times in the Bible we see God working through the hearts of people, especially when choices were made for them by others. Joseph was sold as a slave, Job suffered through loss and pain, and John was beheaded because of a corrupt king. God knows that not all choices are our own, but He has promised He will never leave us nor forsake us (see Hebrews 13:5), regardless of who made the choices that affect our lives.

Walk a different path. Choices will be made with or without you, so choose life through our Father, so that your soul may rest.

#walkadifferentpath

Walk a different path.

Vacations can be so fun. Going to the beach, traveling to the mountains, or visiting a foreign country is exciting for everyone involved, even with the stress of traveling. Whether by car, plane, or boat, journeys in life offer wide possibilities, but sometimes they can also come with fears. Fear of the unknown or of change can make any journey an anxious venture; it can set our hearts to start questioning why we are taking the journey in the first place. This is not just true of our earthly travels, but journeys into new relationships or a new phase in life can leave us timid and afraid that we will be hurt or fail.

God has called us on an incredible journey (see Micah 6:8). He longs to fill our lives with His love, and He calls us to marvel at His wonder. He has created this beautiful planet for us to journey through, but He is just as concerned about the journey of your heart, because He wants that to lead you to Him. God has so much in store for us on our journey, and He wants to hear all about it when we finally make it home.

Walk a different path. If you journey with God all your days, you will never have to ask if you are there yet, for your heart has already gone before you.

#walkadifferentpath

Walk a different path.

I love a good dream. I love being able to see Renae or Mom again, or even—and don't laugh!—fighting side by side with Captain America or patrolling space with the Green Lantern. I also like a good story—one where good triumphs over evil or the good guy gets the girl at the end. Dreams and stories are great, but they are not the reality in which we live. Reality can come crashing down on us like a pounding wave, causing havoc and destruction in its wake. Losing a loved one, losing a job, the kids getting sick, or bad breakups are all part of this thing we call reality. It can bend you and break you to the point that you just want to give up.

Reality is not lost on God. Jesus faced reality in His everyday life, whether from seeing and healing the sick, dealing with unbelief, or, finally, going to the cross that would take His life. God understands that reality can cause us pain, which is why He tells us not to worry because tomorrow has enough trouble on its own (see Matthew 6:31–34). However, He also asks us to believe in Him and He will make our burdens light (see Matthew 11:30). Trust in Him in all things, and He will give you the desires of your heart—in other words, a better reality.

Walk a different path. Reality can bite sometimes, but the reality of heaven is just a whisper away.

#walkadifferentpath

Walk a different path.

I love my children—and I really love the way they got excited today because it was my birthday. The innocence they share is a breath of fresh air every time I am around them. They legitimately want nothing more than my happiness in this life, and that is rare in this world. We have a tendency to let things get the best of us and rob us of the joy we have in life, or worse yet, turn us to focus our hurt and pain inward, until it becomes hard to breathe and going on seems to be not worth the effort.

"The joy of the Lord is [my] strength" (Nehemiah 8:10 NKJV). God put these words in the Bible because He knew there would be hours, days, weeks, months, and sometimes even years when we would walk the line between joy and pain. God reminds us that He is our strength and that we can take joy in the knowledge that even if it doesn't seem like it, He is steering the ship. God wins in the end over everything, and joy will be ours when we finally rest with Him in the place He promised He would build for us.

Walk a different path. Sorrow and pain will come, but joy in the Lord remains to show us of a better place soon to come.

#walkadifferentpath

Walk a different path.

How many times in our lives have we faced disappointment? It may be in how our kids acted, not getting the raise or promotion we worked so hard for, or just overall discouragement in life—disappointment comes in all shapes and sizes. At these times we may wonder, *Am I not a good parent? Am I not worth being rewarded for the work I've done? Am I not worth the effort?* These feelings can overwhelm us, sending us down a hole where inadequacy, resentment, and bitterness take root in our hearts, It can be like trying to stand in the ocean when waves are pounding at our body.

Disappointment is not lost in our Father's eyes. God sees all, and He knows how hard we struggle with these feelings. That is why He is quick to comfort us when life throws us these curve balls. God shows up to remind us that we are never a disappointment to Him, so we shouldn't feel that way about ourselves. We have been "fearfully and wonderfully made" (Psalm 139:14 NKJV), "created in His own image" (Genesis 1:27 NKJV), and yes, all of us are "heirs to the kingdom" (James 2:5 NKJV). You are a son or daughter of the King, and His love for you is not predicated on how hard you work. You are worth the effort, because He died to show you that.

Walk a different path. Disappointments will happen, but when they do, straighten your crown and remember that you can never disappoint His love.

#walkadifferentpath

Walk a different path.

I have the sweetest children. They often just come up to me and say, "I love you, Daddy." Or they will come lie in bed with me, snuggle up, and remind me that they love me. There is no greater feeling in the world than when someone loves you or you feel loved. Skies seem to clear, and the day is brighter when we know someone is thinking of us. When someone calls us just to say they care and share those three words, "I love you," it can speak straight to our hearts and souls. Having your heart touched by someone, whether it be your kids, spouse, or another special person, can lift you up and make your world seem so beautiful.

Our Father is the Author of love, and He wants to share a special bond with each and every one of us. His love is eternal (see Jude 1:21 NKJV), and it never fails because it is not predicated on feelings, but rather on His innate goodness and love for His children. God's love drives out all fear (see 1 John 4:18), chases away the darkest night, and illuminates even the coldest heart. His unfailing love was demonstrated at Calvary, and it continues today with the promise that all tears will be wiped away from our eyes.

Walk a different path. Let God's love capture your heart and know that He thinks you are special and worth dying for.

#walkadifferentpath

Walk a different path.

Some things in life are hard to take. Some things happen to us or are said to us that lead us to a certain place. That place is darkness. Losing a loved one will take you there. Being rejected or told you are not good enough will take you there. Sometimes the way you were raised will take you there. Darkness is greedy; it doesn't care how it gets its claws into you, it relishes your pain and holds you down, leading you to believe that there is no escape, that you have no worth, and that there is no one who cares. It is suffocating, draining the very life from you.

I believe this is why God said darkness and light cannot coexist. Light—specifically, His illuminating Light—pierces through the veil of darkness and lifts us to heights we never dreamed of before. Need examples? Consider Joseph in prison; Moses before Pharaoh; David before Goliath; Shadrach, Meshach, and Abednego in the fiery furnace; Daniel in the lions' den; the disciples and the trials they suffered; and Paul when he was shipwrecked. You get the point. God allows us to experience darkness so that we reach for His light, which is His never-failing love for us (see Psalm 18:28).

Walk a different path. Darkness may try to trap you, but God's unfailing light will illuminate your road so you can see and hope again (see John 8:12).

#walkadifferentpath

Walk a different path.

I remember the feeling when it happened. If I am being completely honest, it seems to happen quite a bit, and I know I am not the only one. Disappointment, that ugly emotion, came into my life, stirring up feelings of dread, anger, bitterness, and resentment. We are disappointed when we don't get a promotion, or we didn't get a new car, or when the relationship we hoped for didn't work out or never materialized. Disappointment comes in all shapes and sizes, capturing our hearts and minds and taking us to some very dark places.

God understands our disappointments and the emotions that come with those unfulfilled desires. However, if He gave us everything we wanted, we would see that everything is not what we need. God supplies all our *needs* according to His will because He can see down the road and around the bend (see Philippians 4:19). He wants us to trust that He knows what is best for our lives and that He would never lead us somewhere that would harm us. His Word clearly states this, that He knows the plans He has for each of us, plans to prosper and not to harm (see Jeremiah 29:11).

Walk a different path. You may get disappointed with life, but He will never disappoints you if you put your trust in Him.

#walkadifferentpath

Walk a different path.

Two emotions can stir the soul like no other. They seem to go hand in hand, as usually one doesn't appear without the other. They can make us feel at our lowest and even have us questioning our lives and the choices we make. *Failure* and *regret* are brothers in arms that can chip away at our self-esteem, our ability to interact with others, and our overall outlook on life in general. Failure will make us think we are not good enough or not worth anything. Regret will remind us of that failure, how we didn't act upon something, or how we did, and now our decision has blown up in our face. Whether it be at a job, in a missed or broken relationship, or in how we see ourselves as spouses, partners, parents, and friends, failure and regret seem to always want to put us in prison and throw away the key.

God never calls us failures. God will never regret calling us His children. No matter what we do, His loving voice is there, reassuring us that we can try again and that there is no need to lie down in the field of regret. God understands that we may try and get frustrated, especially when we fail, but He also knows that in Him we have already succeeded in life because He is our Father and we have been adopted as sons and daughters into His Kingdom (see Romans 8:15). Failure and regret cannot stand against the uncompromising love He gives and the reassurance that He will always be there for us and wipe every tear from our eyes.

Walk a different path. Failure and regret cannot always be avoided, but Calvary shows they have been nailed to the cross.

#walkadifferentpath

Walk a different path.

I really miss being married. I loved that I had that one person on whom I could depend, the one I could share my day with as we spent time together. Loneliness creeps in from time to time, and my heart aches for what was and hopes for what could be. There are others who feel this way, as well, but loneliness can creep in even when you do have a partner. It can reach into your heart at any moment, catching you off guard and shaking your life and your faith. Loneliness can happen at the job site, while you are away from home, or even in the midst of good company, as it is no respecter of any particular person.

Jesus is well-acquainted with loneliness. He was alone in the desert while being tempted, alone in the garden praying while His friends slept, alone as He was beaten and flogged, and finally, alone when He was crucified on the cross. Yes, our Savior is very close to loneliness, but that is what makes Him so easy to relate to. Jesus has felt everything that we have at some point (see Hebrews 4:15), so He can understand our loneliness and seeks to fill that space with His love. Nothing drives out loneliness better than a true display of love and intimacy, and He provides that for us, even when it seems otherwise. He promised He would never leave us nor forsake us, thus proving for all time that we are never alone.

Walk a different path. Loneliness will come from time to time, but Jesus is with you, even unto the end.

#walkadifferentpath

Walk a different path.

I want things. I want my kids to grow up honorable and healthy. I want to do well at my job. I want to be a good father. There are things I don't have that I want. I want to have someone who loves me and my kids, and I want to share that life with someone. Wants are often good; there is usually nothing wrong with them. But there is a difference between a want and a need. Sometimes we want that job, car, house, or partner, and while those things are nice, they are not always what we need.

God knows our wants, and He wants to give us the desires of our hearts (see Psalm 37:4), but He also knows that what we want is not always what we need. He can see down the line, and He knows what heartbreaks can lie ahead when we get what we want outside of His plan for us. It is because of His great love that sometimes His answer is "no," even when we want something really bad, because He has something better in store than what we want at that given time.

Walk a different path. Focus on what God gives that you need, and you will never want for anything.

#walkadifferentpath

Walk a different path.

I have had my share of letdowns and hurt. Shattered expectations and broken dreams. We try every day to be the best humans we can be, but still our hearts get broken, our dreams are crushed, and our spirits feel at their lowest. We work hard at something and pray, and it all falls apart before our eyes.

God is the Comforter when we face shattered dreams. God wants the absolute best for us, and He wants to give our lives such fulfillment. When we trust in Him, we can honestly look at situations where we think our dreams are shattered and realize He has something better for us. His Word says He knows the plans He has for us—and they are for good. If God can create the universe and every living thing in it, He can be trusted to know what is best for us (see Psalm 37:3).

Walk a different path. Trust God with your hopes and dreams because He cares for you.

#walkadifferentpath

Walk a different path.

How many times have you been wronged in your life? Go ahead and count. I'll wait . . . I imagine it has happened many times. Some guy cut in front of you in traffic, or your co-worker stole your yogurt from the break room. Silly, perhaps. But what about even deeper things like getting passed over for the promotion you deserved, or always being the last because you are the youngest sibling, or even having someone break your heart. When these little and big things happen, sometimes we start to think, *This isn't fair*, and that vengeance needs to be taken for our perceived slights and hurts. We can become so consumed with seeking revenge that it blinds us to the damage that we do around us and to our own hearts.

God has clearly said, "Vengeance is Mine, I will repay" (see Romans 12:19). Now, God is not going to strike someone down because they cut in line or "borrowed" your yogurt, but He does deal in justice when it comes to the hurts we face. God tells us we should love our enemies and pray for those who hurt us or seek to cause harm. Even though this can be tough, He will give us the peace we seek if we truly ask with a contrite heart, and He will heal us from the hurts that have been inflicted upon us.

Walk a different path. Revenge is not a dish God wants us to serve to anyone, so trust in His grace and mercy—and hide the yogurt!

#walkadifferentpath

Walk a different path.

Being a widower, father, son, brother, and friend, I have experienced my share of pain and heartache. I have heard my children cry out in pain or sickness, and it tears at my heart. I have seen my family and friends, people I love and cherish, struggle with hurts, loneliness, and feelings that the world is coming to an end, and it rips at my soul. I have been asked to pray for so many people, and I do lift them up, but I know sometimes it can seem there is no relief in sight, that the mountains that are before us seem to cast a deep, dark shadow over our lives, and we spend every day in the valleys of despair. We cry out for mercy and help and listen for a reply or some semblance of a better morning or sunset for our worries and concerns.

God knows exactly how we feel because He became a human being so He could sympathize and relate to each and every one of us (see Isaiah 53). The Bible doesn't mention it, but I am sure there were times when Jesus got sick. There were times when He felt the hunger pains of going without food. I am sure there were nights when He had so many things weighing on His mind, and I am here to tell you, you were at the top of that list. Jesus went through all His trials and suffering just so He could look you in the heart and say, "My child, I understand." His mercy and grace, but most importantly, His love, reaches us in any dungeon or low point in our lives and encourages us to lean on Him, as He will *never* leave us nor forsake us.

Walk a different path. The world can beat you to the ground, but the nail-scarred hands show His love never fails.

#walkadifferentpath

Walk a different path.

I am amazed at how we look at different things. It is kind of like the whole glass-half-full, glass-half-empty scenario. How we see things is all based on our perspective. What an interesting word and action *perspective* is. It can cause us to see the beauty of a flower or a sunset, or experience the calming feeling of rain hitting the roof. But it can also cause us to see hurts that others don't see, that unkind word that takes on a life of its own and even makes us question the way we look at life as a whole. Perspective can be the calm in our storm or the mighty hurricane beating at our walls.

God has a different perspective. From His eyes and point of view, we are worth the whole universe—so much so that He didn't even spare His own Son (see Romans 8:32). See, God's perspective is that He looks beyond how things appear and shows us what they really are. A life free of pain, worry, and doubt, a perspective that sees the heavenly and not the earthly—that's what He died for and why He is constantly reaching out to our hearts to change our perspective and help us see things through His eyes.

Walk a different path. Perspective can be ugly or kind, but it is better to see through a God-shaped lens.

#walkadifferentpath

Walk a different path.

There are things in life that we want. All I have ever wanted was to be a good father and a good husband. Those were really the only things that mattered to me. But what about those things we want most that we can't seem to have? Does our heart break when we try so hard to obtain them but we don't? Or when we pray into the stillness of the night for something to happen or we go out of our way to capture that one thing that will make us happy? Do we rage against everything because we feel cheated and let down?

God loves us, and He wants to give us the desires of our hearts (see Psalm 37:4). His Word clearly states that, but He wants us to seek Him first. He desires to have a relationship with us so that we can truly know what it means to be at peace and to know a love that supersedes any emotion we could ever feel. His love will help us be patient and wait for the day when He reveals to us the wonderful plan He had all along, followed by eternity with Him.

Walk a different path. Sometimes it seems we can't have what we desire most, but God will always give us what we need.

#walkadifferentpath

Walk a different path.

My kids love space. They are enamored by it. I must admit, I think it would be cool to walk on the sun or stand at the event horizon of a black hole and yell into it. The allure of space is based on how vast it is, but what we really know is that space is also a whole lot of empty. Planets may seem like they are close, but there is more empty space than anything else out there. The emptiness stretches on—and the same can be said for the way we feel inside sometimes, as well. We can feel so devoid of anything, and that emptiness we feel in our souls can overwhelm us to the point of pure panic and dread. The feeling of nothingness, of being alone, or of not having a purpose can lead us to question if we will ever be full of anything or whether the emptiness is all there truly is.

God is the cure for this emptiness. He longs to put His enormous love in our hearts, a love that will fill any need or want. A love that will push the emptiness aside and drive it far from our souls. He longs for a relationship that will be eternal, where we can live knowing we are not alone, in that final place of rest that calls to us in our very depths. God fills us, and when He does, the emptiness disappears, and we are changed to experience His eternal love in its place (see Psalm 16:11).

Walk a different path. Emptiness seeks to weaken, but God's presence and love replaces the emptiness with hope and strength.

#walkadifferentpath

Walk a different path.

What does it mean to fall in love? On October 24, 2008, at 7:23 p.m., I fell in love with Renae after just two weeks of dating. I knew she was the one. On June 27, 2014, at 6:57 p.m., I fell in love again. Connor was born, and I fell head over heels in love with him. On November 10, 2015, at 8:57 and 8:58 p.m., yes, once again, I fell in love when Chloe and Matthew were born. I loved my wife, and I still love my kids just as much today as I did the day they took their first breaths. But many people do not get to experience that kind of falling in love, and they long to have a special connection to someone, that deep love in their hearts and souls that shows them they are not alone, that they are worth something to someone.

God is that Person for me above everything else. I am so in love with my Creator, and He is in love with me, so much so that He died for me so we could be together for all eternity. God wants that kind of relationship with each of us because He is the very essence of love. He longs to have that connection with you (see Psalm 36:7). God calls out to you, like a pursuing Father, longing to share all that He is with you, to take you in His arms, to hold you, and to keep you safe from any harm. He wants to bring you to His home and love you forever, because that is what a Father does.

Walk a different path. A spouse and kids are a treasure, but falling in love with Him makes life all the more amazing.

#walkadifferentpath

Walk a different path.

I am guilty. I have no defense. I am guilty of not being the best friend, not being there when I am needed. I am guilty of hurting people, intentionally and unintentionally, by my actions and words. I am guilty of not being the father to my kids they deserve through my lack of patience and understanding. I am guilty of many things in this life, many things I can change, but for whatever reason, fail to do. I am Paul when he says, "The things I want to do, I don't do, and the things I don't want to do, I do. What a wretched man I am." I am guilty (see Romans 7:19–25).

God sees all our failures. His law requires that we answer for our transgressions, but His great love for us stays the guilty verdict due to the sacrifice of His Son on Calvary's cross. God wants us to be with Him in eternity, but He knew that by the law we were guilty, so grace takes the law's place and redeems us to a life everlasting with our Father, the way it was meant to be from the beginning. Jesus sacrificed His life, taking our guilt so that we could be washed clean and have the road home opened once and for all—for everyone who calls His name.

Walk a different path. The gavel may come down, but the voice of God declares, "Not guilty!"

#walkadifferentpath

Walk a different path.

Summer, fall, winter, and spring. Each season has its time and brings its joys and annoyances (see Ecclesiastes 3:1–8). Life is quite the same way, and to everything under the sun, there is a season as well. Unfortunately, many of us feel like we are always in the season of walking alone in the wilderness. We believe we see spring just up ahead, then while walking through the summer heat, we arrive at fall, where all is starting to wither, and eventually we land at winter, where life seems cold and distant, leaving us longing for springtime again. The wilderness is a place that will make the seasons of life seem longer and harder to bear, and it might eventually even make us want to give up.

God did not spare His own Son from the wilderness, nor did He spare Him from the seasons of life. Jesus knew loneliness, He knew hunger, and He knew grief. He faced the same wilderness that we all face. He promises that He understands, and more importantly, that He will be with us and never leave us. Because He understands, we can trust that He will walk us through any season in our lives, especially when we feel alone in the wilderness. Even death cannot stop His unfailing love for us and His willingness to get us home safely to Him.

Walk a different path. Seasons come and go, and the wilderness is vast, but God is our constant Shepherd through the journey.

#walkadifferentpath

Walk a different path.

We have all felt its sting and influence in our lives. Whether it be a sick child, a flat tire, a broken relationship, or a bad day at the office, stress loves to come in and kick us in the gut, letting us know that she is around every corner and in every alley of our lives. Stress does not play favorites, and she really does not care what it does to our minds, our bodies, and our souls. Like a life-draining leech, she latches on, causing us to overthink or do things out of character because of the influence we allow her to have in our lives.

Jesus knows a thing or two about stress. From setting up a ministry, to knowing the hour of His death and having His friends abandon Him, believe me, our Savior is an expert on stress. However, Jesus told us not to let our hearts be troubled because in this life there would be stress, but He promised to be with us and that we could overcome because He did (see John 14:1; 16:33). Stress should not take up any space in our hearts or lives because He has overcome and He tells us not to be afraid.

Walk a different path. Stress will try to sway us to fear, but He has promised that stress is only for a moment and fear has no place in our lives.

#walkadifferentpath

Walk a different path.

"I have long feared . . . that my sins would return to visit me. And the cost is more than I can bear." This line was spoken in a movie years ago, and it is indicative of how many of us feel in our lives. We feel we have messed up so much that eventually those mistakes will come back and rob us of the lives we have built. Like a stalking lion, the past—and moments from that past—seem to be waiting to show themselves and leave us maimed and crippled. We feel we don't deserve to live happy lives because of what we have done or said, and that it is only a matter of time before everything comes crashing down, like a huge tidal wave washing over the land.

But God knows everything we have done and every thought we have ever had. He has not always been pleased with every decision, but that is where it stops. God loves us so much that rather than spend one second without us, He gave up the most precious thing He had—His Son—so we could feel the weight of that sin and regret lifted from us. The Bible says that when He forgives, He remembers our sins no more (see Hebrews 8:12)—and neither should we. As far as the east is from the west, He casts our sins, and seeing as those directions never meet, we can be sure that our past won't return to us, either (see Psalm 103:12). His mighty love covers us and reminds us that we are His and that nothing can separate us from His love (see Romans 8:35–39).

Walk a different path. Past sins can't revisit us when God hurls them into the sea of forgetfulness.

#walkadifferentpath

Walk a different path.

"I would move the mountains for you. I would swim the ocean to get to you. I will love you forever." Sound familiar? I have heard this spoken many times by women and men who were stating their love for each other. They stated they would do the impossible, just for that shot at "forever." The problem is, forever is a long time, and being able to do any of these things is next to impossible. Our view of forever is one-sided, because while we have the best of intentions, we really can't deliver on these promises, and sometimes that can be a letdown.

God specializes in the impossible. Jesus walked on water and raised the dead, but to see forever, we only have to look at His last day on earth and what happened while He was in the tomb. See, Jesus died to take on all our sins, but He saw forever—and not just the moment. He went to hell, kicked down the door, and took the keys to the very things that had separated us from forever, namely, death, hell, and the grave (see Revelation 1:18). He did that so He could forever shatter the chasm between us and God and take away all our fear of leaving earth behind. His love for us supersedes everything else, and He proved that when He rose from the grave, showing us that death has no more hold on us.

Walk a different path. Earthly love is temporary, but Christ invites you to reach for the forever love that God has for you.

#walkadifferentpath

Walk a different path.

Many things go into life. How you act toward someone, where you live, and what type of parent or spouse you will be make up a great deal about who you are. There are so many who believe it takes so much of one thing or another to make one happy, or to fulfill someone's idea of how that life should be. We fool ourselves into thinking that this job, or that partner, or that vehicle will make us the happiest, believing in our very souls that that is what will sustain us and bring us to a place of peace. We spend so much time looking for those things to add on that the peace we crave slips away, and we are left wondering why it wasn't enough.

God should be all we ever need, and He is always enough (see 2 Corinthians 9:8). God wants us to always seek Him because His love is enough to sustain us through any trial that comes our way. God wants to be the ultimate peace in our hearts and the calmness for our souls, not because we deserve it, but because that is His nature and His true purpose for our lives. He longs to be our loving Father until He one day carries us home to live with Him forever.

Walk a different path. Love is always enough, and the cross of Calvary proves it.

#walkadifferentpath

Walk a different path.

Today is very tough for many people. A heaviness lies on our hearts for today due to past events, a tragedy that should never have happened, yet through acts of senseless evil, our hearts were broken, and our spirits were crushed. The memory of 9/11 is and will forever be in our hearts and minds. We are unable to forget and not willing to, as we lost so many lives and a piece of ourselves as a country, as well. That day changed the way we looked at ourselves as we realized, for the first time since Pearl Harbor, that some things were out of control in this world—and that we were vulnerable.

God understands that this day is forever burned into our collective memory, but He also knows that He is still the One in control. This world is bound to His will and not anyone else's, so we can be assured of His grace and mercy. While it may be hard to understand, God grants us the free will to choose, and unfortunately some choose evil. That is where He comes in to hold us in our pain and anguish and gently remind us that He is there and aware of our sense of loss. He pulls us close to Him despite the chaos around us. He is acquainted with sorrow and loss (see Isaiah 53:3), and as our Father, He wants to pull us in and gently whisper, "I love you, and I have you in My hands."

Walk a different path. Remembering this tragic day is certainly necessary, but also remember who always sits on the throne.

#walkadifferentpath

Walk a different path.

I love my children, and I know they love each other, but sometimes they say some mean things to each other, and while they are quick to say "I'm sorry" and forgive, it's not always that easy in the adult world. Sometimes we have been hurt by someone so bad that the pain seems unbearable, and we find ourselves wishing the worst on the person who hurt us. We rationalize that they deserve to be punished because of what they did to us and that justice should be done in the matter. And when that doesn't happen, we tend to think that life is not fair and that they got away with hurting us, which takes us down another path of bitterness and resentment.

God understands that we will not always "be nice" to each other, but He also understands we should forgive one another in love (see Matthew 6:14). We were given a great gift in the redeeming death of Jesus on the cross, a gift we did not earn or deserve, yet it is freely offered to any who will accept it. It's because of the Father's willingness to forgive us for our wrongs that we should be willing to forgive others who hurt us. Jesus had done no wrong, yet He willingly went to the cross to bridge the gap of forgiveness between us and the Father. His life is a great example of ultimate love, one we should reflect in our willingness to forgive others.

Walk a different path. Hurt will come, but our pain is washed away when we walk in His forgiving love.

#walkadifferentpath

Walk a different path.

We are identified quite a bit by what happens to us or how we look. When we lose a spouse, we are "widowed." When we separate from a marriage, we are a "divorcee." When we lose a job, we are "unemployed." The identity we acquire from these situations is not all bad, but sometimes when we are labeled by what happens to us, the truth is, we don't see anything else that we can be. Sometimes identities are placed on us by choices we have made that seem to follow us for the rest of our lives, no matter how much we apologize and make amends. In a negative sense, our identity can have such an impact on our lives that we can see no other person staring at us in the mirror, and our hope for a bright future seems lost in the darkness.

God has a great identity for us. It is not dependent upon what we do, what we say, or how we look. His identity for each of us is "heir to the Kingdom" (see Romans 8:16–17). That's right, we are sons and daughters of the living God, bought with a price and received into His Kingdom to share in eternity. Let that sink in. The same God who formed the stars, the sun, and the planets sees you as the masterpiece that you are, created in His image and loved above all creation. Your identity to Him is the child of the One who did not spare His own Son so you could know what it is to be a child of the King. Jesus said that He went to prepare a place for us, a place where we will live forever with Him and our Father, a place where you will be identified as family in heaven, where you will identified as valued above all else, a place where you can finally rest and be free from any identity placed on you on this earth.

Walk a different path. Identities here can be thrust upon you, but your identity from God comes from the One who longs to bring you home.

#walkadifferentpath

Walk a different path.

I remember many things, especially those that involve my heart. Unfortunately, not all those things I remember are good, and it can be hard to focus on life when those things that shouldn't happen do, especially when we are wounded by those we love or those who claimed to love us. We all tend to have a problem in letting go of the hurt and pain that is inflicted upon us. Letting go—it seems so easy to say, but it is so hard to do sometimes because we want to know why something didn't work or why a certain thing was done or what purpose a certain event served. *Letting go*—two of the hardest words that were ever put together and spoken by anyone who has been hurt or lost something they loved. Letting go . . .

God understands our pain and the hurt we feel when we go through life's unpleasant moments. God wants us to forgive, and yes, just as He forgives and remembers our sins no more, He wants us to forget and let go (see 1 Peter 5:7). See, God knows that holding on to that hurt and pain will cause our hearts to turn hard, and that is not the life He envisions for us. He longs to take us in His arms, He longs for us to rest in Him, while He restores our souls and strengthens our hearts. God does not ignore what happens, but through His love and grace, we can get to the point of realizing that by letting go of our pain, we can truly walk in His light and love.

Walk a different path. Letting go doesn't have to be hard when you leave it at the cross and take His hand.

#walkadifferentpath

Walk a different path.

Sometimes it can be loud. Screaming in your ear, flying down the hill on the seat of your pants, falling from the sky. Sometimes it's subtle. Lurking in the dark like some unknown predator, waiting to spring upon us at a moment's notice. It sends situations like death, heartbreak, anxiety over our jobs, or moves against our family. No matter what it is, life has a way of sneaking in slowly or arriving with a *bang* to steal our peace. We all want peace in our lives—peace to be able to lie down at night and sleep, peace to turn off our minds and stop worrying about this life that has been thrust upon us.

Jesus understood what it meant to have peace. He did not ask the waves if they could politely calm down or maybe be quiet for a minute; He commanded the storm to stop with the words, "Peace, be still" (Mark 4:39 NKJV). See, God is in control of everything, including this life that seeks to take away our peace. He is the King of this world, but more importantly, He is our Father, who seeks to shelter us from life's anxieties and walk us through the storms that will come up in our lives. Before He left this earth, Jesus told us, "Peace I leave with you, My peace I give to you" (John 14:27 NKJV), meaning that we can draw upon that peace for our own lives. Because the same power that raised Christ from the dead lives in us, by His Word, we can have that peace that comes with being His child.

Walk a different path. Life may not care if you are in the gutter, but God will pull you up with His peace that passes all understanding.

#walkadifferentpath

Walk a different path.

Last night was a rough one at our house. A tornado warning was issued, and sirens started blaring. My oldest, Connor, immediately jumped up from bed, screaming as he ran down the stairs. I took him to the bathroom and went to get my twins, Matthew and Chloe, bringing them downstairs into the bathroom, as well. As I heard the fear in their voices and watched them shake in fear, my heart was breaking as their dad. I stood in the doorway of the bathroom and told them it would all be okay, that they didn't need to be afraid. If you have kids, you know this is easier said than done. The fear they felt was real—and they don't need a possible tornado to experience that fear. Fear can show up in all kinds of situations, such as losing a loved one, a tough breakup, a job loss, and for some, just everyday life. Fear grabs us and holds us in chains, leaving us shaking and crying out for help.

God knew there would be times in our lives, valleys we are going through, storms that are raging, that would shake us and cause fear to rise up within us. In these times, He speaks to us in that still, small voice, reminding us that He is the Creator and that this world bends to His will. More importantly, He reminds us that we are His and we were bought with a price; therefore, nothing can ever separate us from His hands. His love and soothing voice reach out through the valleys, taking us to the heights of the mountains, and His voice speaks to the storms in our lives, saying, "Peace, be still." That's when the waves will stop pounding and the rain will stop pouring. As Psalm 56:3 (NKJV) declares, "Whenever I am afraid, I will trust in You."

Walk a different path. Fear can come at any time, but the Word of God is everlasting, and His voice drives out all fear.

#walkadifferentpath

Walk a different path.

Who are you? Who am I? That question gets asked quite a bit in this life. You are a mom, or you might be a dad. In my case, I am a little of both. You are a son or a daughter. You are a friend, a significant other, or a spouse. We are all asked who we are, and we give our responses based upon whatever title we see ourselves holding. While there is nothing wrong with any of those titles, sometimes we look in the mirror, and after all that is stripped away, we ask ourselves, "Who am I *really*?" That is a question that can send us down a path of self-regret, if we are not where we hoped we would be in life. That can be a dangerous path because it can sap our self-worth and make us question every decision we make.

God wants you to know who you are, first and foremost, in His eyes—and that is a child of the King. You are His most precious creation, and nothing can separate you from His love. As the song says, "Resurrection power flows in my veins, too," and that is a promise from God: that the same power that raised Christ from the dead resides in you, as well, so you are a child of His with access to that power (see Romans 8:11). God also says He is with us even unto the end and that Jesus is preparing a place for us, so we will be citizens of heaven for all eternity.

Walk a different path. Who you are in the world is a human, but who you are in His eyes is His divine creation.

#walkadifferentpath

Walk a different path.

We have all been there at one point. On the way to Where I Have Been Boulevard and Where Am I Going? Avenue. Our lives seem to intersect at one of these two points at any given time. We may feel our lives lack direction, that we are spinning along in this world with no thought to where we are, just where we have been and where we hope we are going. A lack of direction in our lives can leave us confused, angry, and sad—all at the same time. We long to know what this life is all about and where we are headed, many times sacrificing where we are now to some hope for a better tomorrow. This lack of direction can cause anxiety to well up inside us and threaten to drown us in a sea of doubt and loneliness.

God is anything but a directionless Creator. God has created each and every one of us with a purpose in this life, and as His Word says, He who created a good work in you will see it through to completion (see Philippians 1:6). This promise is so key in our lives because it shows we are not without direction, but rather we have a loving Father who has ordered our steps and will lead us on "the paths of righteousness for His name's sake" (Psalm 23:3 NKJV). Think about that for a minute. The God of *everything* is walking with you, providing direction in every aspect of your life, just because He loves you and wants you to prosper and live a happy and fulfilled life.

Walk a different path. The roads we walk may seem directionless at times, but God is the Compass who will guide your walk for all your days.

#walkadifferentpath

Walk a different path.

Daylight Saving Time is coming soon, and it will start getting darker earlier in the day. Some people complain about it, and I see their point, but all in all, I don't mind the change of pace. The darkness we experience at this time of year is temporary, but there is a darkness that we face in everyday life at any given time. It could be the loss of a loved one, a broken relationship, the feeling of not being wanted or desired, or any number of things that seek to snuff out the light that is around us, sending us spiraling into darkness, where we feel defeated, cheated, and unloved. In this darkness, bitterness, hopelessness, and loneliness thrive. They threaten to drag our hearts and souls to the very bottom, and they try to keep us locked up in their chains.

God is the God of light who illuminates the darkness in our hearts (see John 8:12). There is a reason shadows flee before the light, and it is the same when our Creator arrives on the scene of our trials, struggles, and heartbreaks. God shows us with His love that we can be overcomers of the darkness that seeks to rule our lives, shining brightly through our souls and reminding us that there is no valley where He will not shine to show the depths of His love for us. Because of His promise and His love, we can stand firm against the darkness that comes and shine with the light of heaven.

Walk a different path. When darkness tries to move in, flip the switch of the Light of the World to chase the darkness away.

#walkadifferentpath

Walk a different path.

It's strange how some things pop into your mind at random times. I was just thinking about the old TV show from the eighties called *Cheers*. The series takes place in a bar, but I am drawn to the theme song: It would feel good to go to a place "where everybody knows your name" and "they are always glad you came." That is really what we are all looking for—not to have our name known, but to have a place where we belong and are accepted, a place in our hearts where we feel we are good enough, where looks do not determine who likes us, where what we have does not determine who our friends are. We all have the longing to belong, whether in a relationship, with our family, with our friends, at work, or just in life in general.

The good news is that we all belong to God. We are always welcome in His presence, and the most awesome part is that He knows each of our names. His Word says that He knew you in your mother's womb, that you are fearfully and wonderfully made, and most important, that you are bought with His blood, shed on Calvary (see Acts 20:28). There is nothing more you need to do to belong to Him as you are already His child and He loves you more than any other creation. God wants to share Himself with each of us. He wants us to know that we belong forever with Him and that nothing can separate us from His undying love.

Walk a different path. *Cheers* is great on television, but all of heaven will be glad you came when you finally get home.

#walkadifferentpath

Walk a different path.

Every morning I get up and wake the kids to get ready for school. Sometimes I go back in my room and get in bed while I check my email, and sometimes I sit on the couch to do this. But without fail, every morning, Connor always comes and snuggles up to me. He puts his arms around me, only wanting to be next to his daddy and spend the first part of the morning with me—and for this, I am truly very thankful. Not everyone gets to experience times like these; in fact, many people start their day alone and cannot see anything to be thankful for in their day-to-day lives. They long for a connection, to find reason to smile in a world that seems to dole out only pain, to feel wanted and appreciated, much like I feel when my son shows me affection in the mornings.

God wants to be that reason for you to be thankful in your life—not because He is a tyrant, but because He has shown that His love for you surpasses anything you could ever hope for. Who else but God would cross an ocean to find you on a deserted island, or reach across the stars to shine a light into the darkness of this world, lifting you up in His strong hands and gently saying, "My child, I love you"? (see Luke 15:4, 7). God is the God of thankfulness because He has made a way for us to stand, even when it seems no one else cares, even when it seems there is nothing to be thankful for. He has shown His faithfulness to do what is right and always demonstrate His love for His children.

Walk a different path. Be thankful in all things, and like Connor, go snuggle up with your Father and start your day with Him.

#walkadifferentpath

Walk a different path.

We have all had that feeling, especially around midday or perhaps in the early evening when we get home from work. We are hungry. We crave food to fill us because we are drained of energy, or for lack of a better way to say it, we just want something to eat. We can get satisfied with eating and feel better physically, but there is a hunger in us all that is not so easily filled. For some, it's a hunger to be wanted, to feel like someone loves you and cares for you, wanting the absolute best for you and making you feel safe. For others, it's a hunger to go further in life, to take a leap of faith into the unknown and experience a lasting joy in their lives. Regardless of the reason, we all hunger and seek to fill that void with temporary solutions, yet we often find ourselves in worse condition than when we started.

Jesus said, "I am the bread of life"; any person who comes to Him will never spiritually hunger again (see John 6:35). He was showing that He understands what it is like to hunger for acceptance, love, and a place of belonging, and He offers to be all those things to us at the same time. He knew what it was like to be physically hungry; hence the feeding of the five thousand. He knew what it was like to be outcast; hence the healing of the demon-possessed man. And He especially knew what it was like to feel alone, hence the cry, "My God, My God, why have You forsaken Me?" Jesus is the ultimate answer to the hunger we feel in our souls because He experienced what it was like to be human and He can sympathize with us in every situation (see Hebrews 4:15). Because of His great love for us, we can come boldly to Him, and He will be the bread to the hunger that is in each of our souls.

Walk a different path. Come to the Father's table and never hunger again.

#walkadifferentpath

Walk a different path.

I love it when my heart tells me I can do something—until, unfortunately, my mind and my body tell me, *Wait a minute*. Case in point, I went to a roller-skating party with my kids and got out on the rink; I did well until the wheels locked up, and I fell on my knee and back. I then went and bowled with my league that night. Why do I bring this up? Because I am now sore and feel a little broken! I will heal—physically—but what about those times when we are broken, not from falls or sports or doing things we really shouldn't, but from the emotional and spiritual falls in life? We lose someone, we have our hearts broken, or better said, life happens. We feel as though we are cut and bleeding inside, and no amount of crying or praying will heal the wound. Brokenness seems to overwhelm us and drag us down to the lowest pits of despair, away from the light, covering our hearts in darkness.

God understands when we feel broken. His Word tells us He is close to the brokenhearted and wounded in spirit (see Psalm 34:18; 147:3). He will never turn away from His child who is hurting and needing a strong hand to lift them up. God is a good Father, and He will pick us up from the dust of our hurts, brushing us off and showing us the love we deserve. He draws us close when we are broken, reminding us that we are never alone and that He is always close to His children, ready to jump into action to protect us and keep us safe. His Word says He will wipe every tear from our eyes, so we can be assured that the God who created the universe is forever in our favor and will welcome us when we fall, offering healing and strength.

Walk a different path. Our God heals all hurts and pain in our lives, even the unfortunate skating incidents.

#walkadifferentpath

Walk a different path.

Sometimes we don't see them when they are right in front of us. Sometimes they pass us by because we are looking for something else even they are slapping us in the face, but we refuse to listen. Taking that trip to a different state or part of the world. Taking that new job and ignoring the fear that is welling up inside us. Taking that risk to ask that person out because we are afraid of rejection. Opportunities are everywhere, just waiting for us to seize them, but many times we are reluctant to do so because of fear of failure or rejection. We stand still where we are, and we never get to experience something new and wonderful, leaving us longing for what might have been or waiting for another opportunity to come along.

God is the Master of opening up new opportunities in our lives. Many times, He is the One who is opening the doors we see, usually something small that leads to a domino effect. We get the new job, which allows us to travel and then meet that special person. God has a perfect plan for each and every one of us (see Jeremiah 29:11), filled with opportunities to have the best life imaginable. His Word clearly says to seek His Kingdom and all will be added unto you (see Matthew 6:33), oceans of opportunities that He intends to use to bless your life abundantly. Why? Because He loves you and wants nothing but the absolute best for you, as any loving Father would.

Walk a different path. When opportunity knocks, open the door to what God has in store for you.

#walkadifferentpath

Walk a different path.

Today is my twins' birthday, and like every other kid on the planet before their special day, they have told me all the things they *want* for their birthday because they think they *need* everything! As their dad, I have to curb some of their wants by limiting their asks and keeping things within reason. This is a normal occurrence, but we also have wants in our lives that we feel we need to sustain our lives. A good job, a healthy body, and a family—a relationship or a marriage—these are all things that we want at any given time in our lives. But what happens when we want something that we feel will make us happy, but it never comes to fruition? That job or raise never comes, a family member gets sick, or the person we wanted to marry has no interest in being with us? When we truly, honestly want something and we don't get it, it can lead us down a path of depression and lack of self-worth, threatening to drown us in a wave of destructive emotions.

God wants us to have the desires of our hearts. His Word even states that He longs to give us those desires (see Psalm 37:4). But He also knows that sometimes those things we want are not always what's best for us. Just as a parent has to rein in their children's birthday requests, God allows us not to get every single thing we want because He wants us to also be grateful for that which we do have. God will always supply our needs (see Philippians 4:19), but we also must trust that He will give us those desires, if they are formed within the right spirit, and in His timing, which is always perfect.

Walk a different path. The desire for things that are pure is not a bad thing, but trust that He will deliver in due time.

#walkadifferentpath

Walk a different path.

I had a friend tell me this morning that we can "create our own noise," and I thought to myself, *And it can get loud!* The noise can make our mind race, thinking about what we need to get done, that deadline that must be met, or that bill that must be paid. That noise can reach into our hearts, gripping us with dread and fear. We worry that no one wants us, that we don't matter, or that we don't have what we need to get ahead. The noise can be loud, especially when we create it ourselves! We struggle to see that it seeks to overwhelm us and keep us locked down, in our own minds or hearts, chained to what we feel are inadequacies or failures on our part.

God is the great Noise Canceller. No matter if the noise is of our own creation or caused by the world, He speaks through the noise in that still, small voice (see 1 Kings 19:12), ever reminding us that He has us firmly in His hand. "If God is for us, who can be against us?" (see Romans 8:31). Those words are in the Bible to remind us that no matter what comes our way, the God of the universe is not swayed or stopped by the noise that seeks to claim our spirits. God is a strong tower to which we can run (see Proverbs 18:10) and escape the self-inflicted noise, as well as the noise that comes from outside sources. God is not bothered by noise, and He is not shaken by events that transpire from its cause.

Walk a different path. The noise in our lives is certain to come, but because He is our Father, we can know that it will fade into the background in His presence.

#walkadifferentpath

Walk a different path.

There is a girl in my life who takes my breath away. She is eight years old, and she always tells me she thinks I am cute when I dress up and that I smell good when I am wearing cologne. My daughter, Chloe, loves her daddy, and I love her unconditionally. This is a father/daughter love, but in life, there is no greater feeling than to be loved by someone, to be told that you matter, that you are missed, that you are desired, that you are important. To know in your life that there is someone rooting for you to succeed and has your back when times get difficult—this can be the difference between a healthy life and one filled with sadness. We all look for that person who fills us with strength, or the ability to just try once more, to look forward to a better day, and to keep trying.

There is no one more in love with you than your Father in heaven. God is always cheering you on because of the undying love He feels for you. There is no distance He will not travel nor any obstacle too big that He can't overcome, just to meet you right where you are. His love is not dependent on what you can do for Him or what you look like. He loves you with an eternal love (see Romans 5:5), such that cannot be measured or quantified on any level that you can truly understand. Hear this: the God of the universe is madly in love with you because *you* are *you*, and that is enough.

Walk a different path. The love of a daughter or a partner is a gift from heaven, but our Father's love is a boundless treasure.

#walkadifferentpath

Walk a different path.

Every night when I put my kids to bed, I pray with them; say "I love you"; and tell them, "Daddy will see you tomorrow." This is a normal activity for many of us. We tell our loved ones we will see them tomorrow, or we will talk to them later. We make plans to go to that concert next month, or take that trip in the summer, with no thought to anything preventing that from happening. We believe we will see those we love the next day and that the plans we make will come to fruition, because we don't envision anything happening that would stop them from taking place.

This is what God means by "faith." We believe we will wake up the next day because, whether we call it that or not, we have faith that will happen. The same is true when it comes to God. He wants us to have faith in waking up tomorrow, but He also wants us to establish that faith in Him to be there for us, to guide us and protect us, and more importantly, to show us the reward for our faith—His undying love. With faith in God, it is easy to see life's problems and know—not *think*, but *know*—we can overcome because we can move those mountains that are in our way (see Matthew 21:21), just by having the smallest amount of faith. He longs to show us the wonders we long for; we just need to believe.

Walk a different path. Lay your head down to rest, knowing that faith in Him guarantees you a happy and fruitful future.

#walkadifferentpath

Walk a different path.

"In brightest day . . ." This is the beginning of the oath of the Green Lantern Corps. (I know—go ahead and laugh!) These words have always stirred my heart because they remind me that there are bright days, and not just blackest nights. Those black nights everyone has experienced, the ones that come from the late-night phone calls, the bad news at work, the person who leaves? We have all seen and felt the weight of those nights invading our lives, and it becomes hard to see the brighter days ahead when we are constantly pounded by waves of grief, betrayal, and hurt.

"In brightest day . . ." is God's promise to us. His Word says we will walk through the valley (see Psalm 23:4), the blackest nights, but that He will be with us when we do. God will be with us when we stand against the giants, He will be with us when we face the approaching armies, and He is with us when we approach the fiery furnace. See, God wants you to know that He is with you even unto the end, that His love will carry you, and even when you think the night is the blackest, you are merely moments from the brightest day He has in store for you (see Proverbs 4:18).

Walk a different path. In brightest day and in blackest night, you will never be far from His sight.

#walkadifferentpath

Walk a different path.

Thankful. What does it mean to be thankful, and why does it matter? I am truly thankful that I have my children; all three of them put smiles on my face daily. I am thankful for the fact that I have a roof over my head and I can provide for my children. But what about those times when we don't feel so thankful? We might lose a job, we might get in an argument with a family member, we might break up with that special someone, or in some cases, we might even lose that person who is most precious to us. We can get so deep into the hurt and pain that it's hard to see those things for which we should be thankful in everyday life. The sorrow from life's constant hits can drive us like a stake into the ground, causing us to lash out, or even worse, shut down inside and hide away from everyone and everything.

"Blessed are the poor in spirit, for theirs is the kingdom of heaven" (Matthew 5:3 NKJV). Yes—read that again. When our spirits are down and we can't see anything to be thankful for, God reminds us that He loves us and that we have a share in His Kingdom. Think about that for a minute and let it soak in. God cares so much for you that He wants you to know that even when you are feeling poor in spirit, you are still an heir to heaven. Thankfulness is driven from this promise because it shows that no matter what, we are still held by a loving God and His abiding promise. God wants us to be thankful in all things and circumstances (see Psalm 100:4), even when it seems hard, because He can see the road up ahead and He knows our true destination and purpose.

Walk a different path. When you see the promise waiting for you, being thankful will come naturally to you.

#walkadifferentpath

Walk a different path.

"The island of misfit toys." This phrase has been echoing in my mind the last few days. Maybe it's because *Rudolph* was on TV, I don't know, but it has been fresh in my thoughts. Sometimes we can feel like those toys—unwanted, unappreciated, and unloved. Maybe we don't feel good enough, or we don't feel we are pretty/handsome enough, or we feel we don't have anything to offer. Whatever the reason, this feeling of being unwanted can affect us emotionally, but it can also drain us physically and spiritually, as well. We start looking at the many ways that we perceive that we are not needed or wanted, and we start to drift toward that dangerous place of depression, being sucked into that black hole where there is no light and seemingly no hope.

If this is happening to you, rest assured that there is a God who wants you and loves you more than you could ever fathom or calculate (see 1 John 3:16). God specializes in taking what the world sees as unwanted and using those as an instrument for His purpose. He sees us for who we truly are—precious in His sight, beautiful in every way, and fearfully and wonderfully made (see Psalm 139:14). We don't have to be the best at anything, be the best-looking, or have anything to offer, because He asks only for our heart—and that is enough, regardless of the shape it is in. His love and longing for us is not contingent on anything other than us reaching out to Him and allowing His hands to pick us up and guide us as we walk toward eternity with Him.

Walk a different path. The island claims unwanted toys, but there is no island too remote where God will not claim you as His child.

#walkadifferentpath

Walk a different path.

There is nothing quite like a good story. The hero swoops in at the last minute and saves the day. The guy gets the girl in the end, and they live happily ever after. The girl lands that dream job and the guy she has always wanted. Stories reach into our hearts and show us the good things in life and what can happen when we walk the true and noble path. However, life is not like all the stories we see at the movies or on television. Life has its own story, and sometimes it can be cruel and disappointing for many of us. We seem to lose more than we win, and we look to drown ourselves in the emotions that wash over us when things go south and we feel dejected by everyone and everything around us.

However, God is writing a story in this world that is never going to turn out bad. God is creating the story of you. Yes, you—sitting there reading these words. God loves you with such a fierce devotion that even though there are bumps in the road, your story will inevitably have a happy ending—because of who is writing the plot. God seeks to show you the best version of yourself, using you and your story to uplift others and inspire hope in those around you. You are the star of your story because you are the child of the living God, the One who knows every chapter and line and who has detailed it specifically with you in mind (see Psalm 139:16).

Walk a different path. Stories are awesome, but "The Story of You" is His grand masterpiece.

#walkadifferentpath

Walk a different path.

I have never really slept well most of my life. I'm not sure why, and I have tried many remedies. This leaves me tired quite a bit, until eventually my body says, "Enough," and then I crash and sleep. I will eventually solve this issue, but there is another tired in our lives that seems worse than a lack of physical sleep. It's the tired that comes from a lack of peace, the tired that is emotional, the tired you feel deep in your soul. It is a heaviness that weighs on you because you feel like you are drifting through life with no hope, or that no one cares. You feel it in your very soul, and it casts its long shadow over your life, making you feel less than what you should be. You are just tired—of mistakes, of trying, even of breathing.

God understands that we get tired spiritually and emotionally. His Word states that He is the strength of our hearts and our portion forever. He gives strength to the weary and increases the power of the weak (see Isaiah 40:29, 31). These promises are not in His Word for show, but to demonstrate that He loves us and that He will give us the strength we need to drive the tired out of our lives. God wants us to live a fruitful and prosperous life, and He knows that some days try to steal that from us, which is why He lovingly reminds us, "I am with you until the end." He will always remind us of His love when we look toward the cross of Calvary.

Walk a different path. Tired souls are set free when He who never tires gives them rest in Him.

#walkadifferentpath

Walk a different path.

"A day that will live in infamy." Over eighty years ago, we were attacked at Pearl Harbor, losing over two thousand lives in a sneak attack on our own soil. Many movies, television shows, and books have been written about the event and our entrance into World War II. While these kind of attacks are not commonplace, attacks upon our person, and particularly on our hearts, happen every day. We can be hurt by words said to us or stories told about us. We feel hopeless when we are attacked, and we long for rescue, feeling as though we have been left stranded on a deserted island with no means of escape or hope.

God is a strong tower and our stronghold (see Proverbs 18:10). His Word says the righteous run into that tower and are saved. God understands there will be days when we feel the world is against us, when our faith, our convictions, our heart, and even our very lives can be threatened. God's Word also states that no weapon formed against us will prosper (see Isaiah 54:17) and that "if God is for us, who can be against us?" (Romans 8:31 NKJV). God loves you, and He will fiercely protect you against all enemies who come to your door, including the door to your heart. We are His children, and like a good Father, He defends His own and keeps them safe.

Walk a different path. Pearl Harbor was attacked unexpectedly, but nothing surprises the God who is our Father.

#walkadifferentpath

Walk a different path.

Everyone has felt this way before. It is something that happens to each of us at one time or another. We work hard at our job, putting in long hours and going above and beyond, and then someone else gets the promotion. We do everything in our power to be good children, helping where needed and being as supportive of our parents as we can, yet they still don't treat us like parents should. We love our spouse with all our heart, sacrificing our own desires to make them happy, yet they still walk away. This feeling, which we all experience, is the feeling that *I'm just not good enough*. No matter what we tried or did, the outcome was the same, and the feeling of *we are just not good enough* is stamped on our hearts.

God's very Word states that we are a chosen people, God's holy possession (see 1 Peter 2:9). You don't have to be "good enough" in His eyes because you were bought with a price (see 1 Corinthians 6:20), and His love for you supersedes any notion that you are not enough. The world would tell you that you must excel at everything, but God only wants your heart—He will take care of the rest. He has promised that He will support you by feeding and clothing you; that He will be the love that never walks away; and more importantly, that He is a Father who is so proud of the man or woman you are because you are His.

Walk a different path. You are good enough for the King; the world is not worthy of you.

#walkadifferentpath

Walk a different path.

There is a feeling that runs through us, seemingly every day, or at least on a consistent basis. We long for acceptance by the people around us, or we long to see that long-lost friend or relative, or we long to experience that special relationship, and for some of us, we long for that which we have lost. We are human, and that longing is a part of the spirit that is within us. We can feel unfulfilled when that longing persists in our lives. Sometimes we long for something so deeply that it makes us feel debilitated inside and without hope, searching for answers to satisfy that need within us.

No one understands longing more than our heavenly Father (see 2 Peter 3:9). God longs to be a part of our lives, so much so that He crosses any chasm, any ocean, any distance, just to meet us at the point of our greatest need and satisfy that longing in our souls. In His eyes, you are worth more than anything in all creation, and His desire to be in your life and hold you close to Him is a testament to His everlasting love for you. God only wants the best for each of us, but most importantly, He wants us to know what it's like to be a child of the King, a King who only longs for the sons and daughters whom He created.

Walk a different path. We long for many things, but imagine a Creator who longs only for you—just because you are His.

#walkadifferentpath

Walk a different path.

Sometimes life is really hard. Obstacles get thrown in our way. Bills pile up, traffic is bad, the kids get sick, and breakups happen. We look around and throw our hands in the air because it is so hard to believe that it will get better, because the constant sledgehammer of disappointment, failure, and life in general keeps pounding at us slowly and methodically every day. Belief seems to fade into the background of our hearts, and we question what we are trying to accomplish or what this life even has to offer us anymore. The beating that we take over and over again wears down our belief in a fulfilling and happy life and leads us into the realm of heartache time and time again.

"While you were still in your mother's womb, I knew you." God included this in His Word to show you that even before you came into the world, He knew exactly who you were. Think about what is written here and grasp that a loving Father knew who you were before you ever drew breath, and that same Father knows the path you will walk. If He knew you then, He knows how to bring you through the trials you face on a daily basis. God is a strong tower and a refuge that we can take shelter in from the storms of this life and He will stop the constant pounding from life because He is the very bread of life and will sustain us, even through the difficult and treacherous times we face. "God is for us, so who can be against us?" These are not just words in the Good Book, but it is the very Word that will shoulder our burdens and fight against any adversary that would threaten His child.

Walk a different path. While you may feel shaken in life, God believes in you, and that belief will never be shaken (see Psalm 112:5–6).

#walkadifferentpath

Walk a different path.

Heartbreak comes in many shapes and sizes. Your team loses the big game, you lose a pet, a breakup happens—no matter what causes it, heartbreak happens to everyone at some point. Heartbreak hurts, but as the saying goes, "anything broken can heal." It's not the same with heartbreak's sister, heartache. Heartache is different in that it leaves you feeling numb and cold inside, sick to your stomach, with a never-ending throbbing in your chest that consumes your thoughts and your life, sending you down a path of loneliness and despair. Heartache is no respecter of persons; she comes for all of us at some time in our lives, and she wants to stay rooted in us, leaving us feeling like there is no hope or way out, that we are just stuck in our pain.

God is familiar with both heartbreak and heartache. He watched as His own Son was crucified for no crimes committed, and He turned away in heartbreak when Jesus took all our sins upon Himself. God loves us so much that He was willing to endure that heartbreak just to bring us back to Him. His heart aches for us to return to Him, not because He is all-powerful, but because He is all-loving. He knows we will suffer heartache, and He wants to help us overcome the sadness that follows by showing us that there is hope (see Psalm 130:5). God will pick us up from the depths of heartache and show us the path we need to walk—a path that leads to a better future and a brighter, more fulfilling life.

Walk a different path. The two sisters of heartbreak and heartache will come in this life, but your Father will hold you close to heal both the break and the ache.

#walkadifferentpath

Walk a different path.

Have you ever wondered how Jesus was perceived by the people around Him before He met with John at the Jordan River? My favorite author, Max Lucado, wrote in one of his books about the first miracle that Jesus performed at the wedding in Cana. Jesus was invited to the wedding, so we can see that He was liked by many people before He started His ministry—which is key, because it shows His human side. He was invited to the wedding, so surely He must have had friends, right? (see John 2:2).

God delights in letting us know how much He loves us, but the Creator of the universe also *likes* us. He may not like our choices, but I believe He shows, through the stories of Jesus, that He loves us and *likes us* so much that He wants nothing more than to spend eternity with us. Let that sink in. He loves you, but He also likes you. Not who you will be or who you were, but who you are. Do you feel special yet?

Walk a different path. God loves to call you son or daughter, and He likes you also—He is our true Friend.

#walkadifferentpath

Walk a different path.

Last night was really rough. I had a terrible dream involving Matthew. I remember so vividly in the dream how helpless I felt with the situation in the dream. When I woke up, I remembered it was a dream and that my son was safe in his bed. While that was a bad instance, many of us go through life feeling helpless—like, no matter what we try, we cannot seem to get ahead or stay afloat. We lose a job and the bills keep coming; we try as hard as we can, and someone we love still walks away; or sometimes, life itself just drags us down into the murky waters of despair, and we are helpless to stay above water.

The Word states that God takes the side of the helpless, that when we are at the end of our ropes, He saves us (see Psalm 10:14). God never promised that life would not have its bad moments—we know we will feel defeated sometimes—but He did promise that He is with us and that we can overcome because of His great love and strength. See, God understands that we will struggle from time to time, but because He promises to save us, we can know without a doubt that no matter what comes our way, we have a Father who already is fighting the battle for us, and we know that God never loses a battle.

Walk a different path. It may seem that we are helpless, but God fosters a life of hope, one in which we always have a helping hand.

#walkadifferentpath

Walk a different path.

Sometimes it is hard to hear some things, especially when it is from someone whom we love and respect. I have a friend who is really going through it, and as we spoke, I could hear the pain in his words. His frustration was warranted, just as was his pain, but it was the silence that was deafening. We all can relate to this—to the silence that comes when our hearts are breaking, when our whole world is crashing around us, when our souls cry out for help, only to hear nothing in the darkness, no word of comfort, no rescue at the last moment. Our spirits are crushed, and we feel so alone and unwanted, cast away like yesterday's trash, and we sink further into the sadness that carries us away on waves of anger and loneliness, with no sight of hope on the horizon.

Even though we might not want to see it, God completely understands our frustration over this perceived silence from heaven. He gives us many examples of people who have waited for a response from Him, an answer to their heartfelt cries. Abraham and Sarah waited for Isaac, Joseph waited in prison, the Israelites waited in Egypt, David waited to be king, Simeon waited to see his Savior, Mary and Martha waited to see Lazarus raised, and Jesus waited in the Garden of Gethsemane. God uses these examples to show that He is faithful—because the promise of a nation came to bear, that nation was saved from famine, deliverance came to that nation, a giant fell and a king was crowned that established a lineage, a man held his joy and salvation in his own arms, women saw their brother come back to life, and a world was saved through a Lamb's sacrifice. God listens to every one of our requests and prayers, and He is working; we just need to understand that His plan is perfect, and in His timing, our joy will be restored (see Psalm 27:14).

Walk a different path. Silence is not always golden, but His promises and plans are pure gold.

#walkadifferentpath

Walk a different path.

Personally, I like spring. I like seeing the bloom of flowers and the renewal of the trees and the warmth that comes to the air. Some people like summer, others like fall, and some even like winter, but everyone has a favorite season. Seasons show change in the world, but seasons also take place in our lives. Some seasons are great—we start a new job, move to a new city, or find a new love. Some seasons are hard—we get sick, feel lonely, or lose someone we love. Seasons often happen in waves, and there is no timetable for any particular season in our lives, which can bring joy, but that can also frustrate us, depending on what season we are in.

"To everything under the sun there is a season" (see Ecclesiastes 3:1–8). God included these words in the Scriptures because He knew we would question some of the seasons in our lives. God knows that not all seasons are pleasant, but He also knows that not all are crippling either. The purpose of the seasons in our lives is to strengthen us when times are hard and to teach us to be thankful when times are good. As the Word says, there is a time to cry and a time to laugh, a time to grieve and a time to dance. God is with us in every season of our lives, holding us close when we are struggling and rejoicing with all of heaven when we are happy and succeeding.

Walk a different path. Seasons come and go, but God's presence in those seasons of life is a constant reminder of His love for us.

#walkadifferentpath

Walk a different path.

Bottles are used many different ways. Some bottles are for a baby to drink from, others are for water or soft drinks, and some are meant to carry food such as soup. There is nothing like having a full bottle of something refreshing or nourishing readily available. But there are also those spiritual and emotional bottles that we carry. Some of these run over with anger, maybe due to someone wronging you. Some run over with loneliness because maybe that person you loved left or that special someone hasn't come along. Some run over with anxiety due to not knowing where your next meal is coming from or whether there will be enough money to pay all the bills. And yes, there is that bottle of fear, the one that holds our nightmares and mortality within its shape, causing us to be afraid to start over, keep going, or just live life in general.

God knows all too well about the bottles we carry. He understands that we get angry and feel we were wronged, yet He demonstrates grace to us rather than the wrath we deserve. He understands the loneliness because He longs to be with us, just as we long to be with others. Jesus comforts us in our anxiety by showing us that He asked if the cup could be passed when He prayed in the garden. And He certainly comforts us by reminding us not to be afraid, for He is with us to the end. All these bottles are accounted for when the psalmist states, "You number my wanderings; put my tears into Your bottle; are they not in Your book?" (Psalm 56:8 NKJV). God Himself states that He will wipe every tear away and that all the bottles we carry will be emptied and our burdens lifted.

Walk a different path. Our bottles are many and are heavy and overflowing, but God empties the hurt and pours Himself into us.

#walkadifferentpath

Walk a different path.

Like most parents, I love my children with all my heart. I cried when they were born, and I am totally devoted to being their dad. Devotion to one's kids should come naturally, but what about devotion that may be lacking? We may feel like we are devoted to something only to have that devotion not be returned. We may work late hours to get ahead and stay committed and devoted to our careers, only to be let go because someone else can be hired at a lower wage. We stay devoted to our partner/spouse, only to have that devotion repaid with betrayal or worse. This life is full of twisting turns, and our devotion can be pulled in so many different directions that we cannot see what we were truly devoted to in the first place.

This world may sway in the area of loyalty and devotion, but our heavenly Father does not. Need proof? Take that breath of air that you need to survive; He provided that. Look at the roof over your head; He gave that as well. But more importantly, take a look at Calvary, where God sent His Son to die because He couldn't bear the thought of spending eternity without you. Yes, you, reading these words right now—He did that for you because of His steadfast devotion to you. His love reaches through time and space and says He will not give up on you—never will He leave you, and He is devoted to getting you safely home to Him.

Walk a different path. We are devoted to people and things, but His devotion shines through at the cross and in the promise of a forever home (see Romans 5:8).

#walkadifferentpath

Walk a different path.

I don't usually share information about my health, but something unique about me is that I have low blood counts. While this is not life-threatening, it is something that causes cuts in my body not to heal as fast as those of a normal person, which leaves me with scars. I sometimes wonder if this is also what happens to our hearts. So many things happen to us that shake us to our core, things that shape our attitudes about life and the ability to see better days ahead. Losing a spouse or a family member, being betrayed by a friend, being sold out by that close coworker, or being forgotten by our loved ones can leave cuts on our hearts, and the slow healing can lead to scars on our souls, robbing us of joy in life and threatening every part of our future selves. We watch as the scar scabs over, and sometimes we pick at it, releasing the pain of the hurt once again and never allowing the healing to take place.

The late Christian singer Jonathan Pierce once sang, "Pick up your heart and carry it to healing hands." Those "healing hands" he speaks of are the same hands that carry the scars that purchased our salvation and healing. Jesus took thirty-nine stripes on His body, stripes taken for our healing (see 1 Peter 2:24). The scars He received were not just for our physical healing, but they also go deeper, because God knows that emotional and spiritual healing are just as important. Our Father wants to take us in His arms and heal our hurts because He understands what it's like to suffer. He knew hunger; He knew loneliness; He knew loss; and it's because He experienced these emotions that He is qualified to meet us right at the point of our need, extending those healing hands and putting our hearts back together again.

Walk a different path. Low blood counts can slow our physical healing, but nothing stops the healing hands of our loving Savior.

#walkadifferentpath

Walk a different path.

It has been said many times that there's always a price to pay, or there's a cost to everything in life. While this is true in a many things, sometimes it seems the cost is too steep. We try to be a good friend, yet we can be betrayed, costing us the trust we once gave. We can open our hearts to a romantic partner, only to have them hurt or abandon us, thus costing us the ability to look for love again. Or worse, we can just shut ourselves out due to a loss, costing us the ability to live a fulfilling life. The cost of life wears on each of us, and no one is immune to the scars it leaves.

While life seems to extract a heavy cost many times, God is always in the midst of the tragedies that affect us. He is that Friend who calls when it seems that all is slipping away. He is that voice we hear in the darkness when it seems all is lost. And He is that feeling in our souls when we think there is no love for us in this world. God understands what cost is because He gave His own Son to rescue us from this life that demands so much but seems to give so little. Jesus took all the cost on His own shoulders so we could approach the throne of grace, knowing we would be welcomed as sons and daughters and not someone who has a debt to pay.

Walk a different path. There is a cost to many things, but the cost for your heart and soul has been paid in full (see 1 Corinthians 6:20).

#walkadifferentpath

Walk a different path.

They can sneak up on you, and if I'm being totally honest, they have snuck up on me in the past few months. Sometimes they're good; sometimes they're bad. The smile of a child or the start of a new job can bring feelings of love and hope. Unfortunately, we seem to always have more bad than good. Feelings can catch you off-guard if you're not paying attention. When that person doesn't give you the time of day, that's the feeling of rejection. When we tragically lose someone we love, that's the feeling of loss. When a friend we trust turns away, that's the feeling of abandonment. On and on feelings can go, leaving us questioning why we have to go through so much and why we can't just shut it all off. We believe no one understands how we feel, and we suffer in our misery, allowing our feelings to have free rein in our hearts and minds, slowly draining the life out of us.

No one understands feelings more than our Savior. He understands what it's like to have a friend betray you, as evidenced by Judas. He understands what it's like to have a friend turn away, because Peter denied Him three times. He understands what it is like to lose someone, as His cousin John was beheaded. But most importantly, He understands what it's like to be rejected, because He was rejected, beaten for no crime, and nailed to a cross. Jesus felt all our feelings, but despite all the pain, humiliation, and rejection, He still willingly went to the cross for us, because He knew He couldn't resist the feeling of His love for us. He said that no one could take His life, but that He laid it down willingly, so He could bridge the eternal gap between us and our holy Father (see John 10:17–18).

Walk a different path. Feelings can hurt and they can inspire, but what's best is to get lost in the arms of a Savior whose feelings for you are eternal.

#walkadifferentpath

Walk a different path.

I am not ashamed to say that most nights I go to bed with tears in my eyes. This is not because I am sad all the time, but maybe something bad has happened to a friend of mine, or maybe I am crying happy tears because of a good memory. I know I am not the only one who has these moments, and that is okay, as well. We can shed tears because of the birth of a child or a new relationship, just as we can shed tears of despair due to a great loss or a broken heart. Tears come in all shapes and forms from an emotional standpoint, and they can soak our hearts and souls just as easily as they do our faces and pillows.

There is One who sees our tears and draws in close to comfort us. An old song says, "Fear not, My child. I hear every pain, and every tear I see." God is so observant when He hears our cries, and the psalmist states that they are in His record book. God knows there will be times of rejoicing and tears of joy, but He is also aware there will be periods of despair and bitter tears of sorrow. He has promised to wipe every tear from our eyes (see Isaiah 25:8) and that He will collect and remember each one (see Psalm 56:8). The same hands that formed the universe will hold you in His arms and dry the tears from your eyes.

Walk a different path. Tears will fall in our lifetime, but as our good Father, God will restore our souls and brush the tears away.

#walkadifferentpath

Walk a different path.

I am trying so hard as a dad to instill a sense of courtesy in my kids. I always want them to say "excuse me" before walking in front of someone, hold doors open, and not be too loud at a restaurant. These actions may seem trivial to some, but I believe they will build great character in their lives. While it is assumed that everyone should have courtesy, many times we get hurt because others do not show the same courtesy we expect, especially those we care about. Someone doesn't return a phone call or text, or call to say they are running late, or even worse, doesn't show up at all. We all experience these things in our lives, and they can cause us to be bitter because we feel disrespected and unappreciated.

God loves all His children, but we must also realize that He gives us free will to choose. He knows some people will not be courteous to us, but still we are called to love them regardless of the missteps that are taken. See, in our lives we have not always been a shining example of a good person, and yet He forgives us for those instances, so shouldn't we be able to forgive others when we feel that they have not been as good to us as well? Many times Jesus asked, "How long must I put up with you?" (see Matthew 17:17)—not as a negative statement, but rather as a plea to believe and love each other as He has loved us.

Walk a different path. Courtesy should not be difficult; we just need to look at the example He set and follow suit.

#walkadifferentpath

Walk a different path.

We all have this happen from time to time. When we were younger, we fell off our bikes, or out of our beds, or off the monkey bars. We have all had the dream where we were falling and woke up suddenly before we hit the ground. And everyone has fallen in love at some point in their life, as well. We fall a lot in life—physically, emotionally, and spiritually—and it definitely leaves its mark, on the body, the heart, and the soul. We get bruises and scars, and sometimes the healing can take a few days, but it can also take years at times, especially when it comes to the emotional and spiritual falls we take.

God sees us when we fall, and He understands the pain those falls cause. His Word states that He took the stripes for our healing (see Isaiah 53:5), which is most associated with physical wounds, but that can also be interpreted as taken for those scars on the inside that He can see. He longs to pull us close and comfort our hearts, seeking to repair the damage that has been done when we fall and get hurt inside, just as He seeks to heal us physically from our ailments. By our faith and belief in Him we can know He is the ultimate Healer of all wounds we incur from our falls in life.

Walk a different path. Falling down is unavoidable, but there is One who knows how to pick us up, dust us off, and heal all our broken parts.

#walkadifferentpath

Walk a different path.

Many times it has happened, that feeling that you get when nothing is working out and no one seems to care. That sadness that envelops your heart, and the voice in your head that screams at you that it has happened again. I have felt it, and I know I am not the only person who has. The feeling of being abandoned or cast away can torture a soul, making you think you are worth nothing and that there is no happy ending in sight, no matter how many people tell you it isn't true. This feeling weaves its way into your heart and threatens to chain you to a life of sadness and bitterness, eating away at your existence.

The psalmist writes that "even if my mother and father abandon me, the Lord will hold me close" (see Psalm 27:10). These are some of the most beautiful words ever written, because they show us that no matter who might abandon us in this life, God never will. His love for us stretches across space and time, meeting us right at the point of where we feel cast aside and reminding us that we are His children, His arms are around us, and we can run to His covering and be safe. No matter who we have in our lives, or who has cast us aside, He promises to sustain us. This can drive any sadness or fear away and bring us to a life where we belong.

Walk a different path. Whenever you feel abandoned or cast aside, seek the One who always delights in you and laid His life down to prove it.

#walkadifferentpath

Walk a different path.

There are many things I want to be. I long to be a good friend, one who will always be there when others need me, ready to help in any way I can. I want to be an awesome brother, being my brother and sisters' keeper in all things and forever being loyal. I want to be a good son, one whom my dad can be proud of and one whom I know my mom would be as well. I want to be the best father to my kids, showing them the right way to show honor and love. I want to be a good partner in the future, putting my spouse's needs above my own and striving to be the best husband for her. There are many things I want to be, but it's the things I don't that seem to take up space in my head and weigh my heart down. I strive not to let those distractions and thoughts rule me, but they seem to always creep into the front of my mind, and I am sure I am not the only one.

We were not intended to be ruled by that which we do not want to be. The apostle Paul even stated that what he wanted to do, he didn't, and what he didn't want to do, he did (see Romans 7:15–24), so God is aware that we battle against this daily. God wants to give us peace in our lives, which is why He tells us to come and He will give us rest and that we should cast all our cares on Him. God, more than anything, wants us to bring the behaviors, thoughts, or actions that we know we don't want to do and lay them at the cross of Calvary. He also tells us to leave them there and walk away, not to come back for them, but to leave them where they lay. The blood that was shed washes over those things we strive not to be and points us to a brighter and more complete life with Him, free of those things that would seek to destroy us.

Walk a different path. Many things we long to be and many things we don't, but we can always know that we are His forgiven children, and that is enough for Him.

#walkadifferentpath

Walk a different path.

A feeling sometimes wells up in us that can be just as devastating as any slap in the face or push down the stairs. Some people—including myself at times—experience this feeling, and when it isn't fulfilled, we feel cheated or wronged. It's the feeling of "deservedness." *I deserve to get that promotion because I have been here the longest and I work harder than anyone.* Or: *I deserve that new car because I have driven this old pile of parts long enough.* Or: *I deserve that girlfriend because I am a good person and I know I can treat them right.* Deserve, deserve, deserve—it's the distant cousin of pride. *I deserve this and that, and if I don't get it, then the world is against me, and it's not fair.* That might sound like the words of a petulant child, but if we are honest, that how we feel when we think we deserve something and don't get it.

God understands that we work hard and that we want to be appreciated and rewarded when we do good work. Wanting a promotion, a new vehicle, or someone to love—these are all good things in general when they are tempered with humility and patience. But maybe God doesn't want you to have that specific promotion because the company may be shutting down in a year. Maybe God doesn't want you to get that particular car because the salesman is not being honest about the mileage and engine. Maybe God doesn't allow you to be with that person because even though they are His child, as well, He knows they are in a place where they may hurt you and break your heart. His Word says to seek His Kingdom and all its glory first, and then all these things will be added (see Matthew 6:33). God wants us to walk side by side with Him so He can give us not only what we need, but that which we truly deserve.

Walk a different path. We may deserve many things in our minds, but remember that love took our place at the cross so we could receive eternal life.

#walkadifferentpath

Walk a different path.

We all want them in our lives. As a matter of fact, it is probably a good bet to say that we all *need* them in our lives. Those good relationships—whether it be with friends, family members, or romantic partners—everyone wants to have them in their world, those people who make us feel special and who support us. But how many times do we feel we are lacking in this area, that we do not have those people who "get us," or worse, the we have allowed something or someone to tear those relationships to shreds? Maybe a misunderstanding, something taken out of context, or worse, words or actions purposely said or done, make us lose faith in that person and sever the ties of friendship and love, leading us down a path of bitterness.

According to the Bible, there is a Friend who sticks closer than a brother (see Proverbs 18:24). This Friend it speaks of is our Father in heaven. God can be our best Friend in life because, more than anything else, He wants to see us happy and living a fulfilling life. He is our family, in that He is our Father, and every good father strives to give the very best to his child, just like God does for us. And as far as romance—how can you not see the love He has for each of us? God's love for us is immeasurable, and He pursues us daily, longing to draw us close to Him in the greatest love story ever told: His offering of grace and mercy, and more importantly, forgiveness for all we have done.

Walk a different path. Relationships can be tricky and delicate, but the love story that is being written about you and your heavenly Father is the relationship of a lifetime.

#walkadifferentpath

Walk a different path.

We have all faced the question of "What's next?" or "What happens now?" Usually, this question seems to come after something life-changing has happened to us, be it good or bad. When we retire, we ponder, *What do I do now? Do I travel, move to Florida, or just sit back and relax?* When a close friendship dissolves, we wonder, *Where do I go for advice? Who can I call and talk to or hang out with?* When a romantic relationship ends, we may question, *Why did this happen? What did I do wrong?* Or even worse, *Am I unlovable?* Finally, when someone we love passes away, we ask, *Why did this have to happen?* And, *How can I fill this emptiness that is in my heart now?* Many questions fill our minds and cause us to look around and wonder what we see and feel. This can create anxiety or fear in our souls, which then sends us down the road to uncertainty.

"For I know the plans I have for you, plans to prosper you and not to harm you, plans to give you hope and a future" (Jeremiah 19:11 NIV) These words are straight from God's Word, and they are so important to remember in our daily lives. See, God understands that there is uncertainty in our lives, times when things don't make sense, times when we might even question whether He is listening. These words show us that despite everything that happens, He has a plan. Retiring and not sure what to do? He has a plan. Lose a friendship? He has a plan, and He sticks closer than a brother. Get your heart broken in a relationship? He has a plan, and He loves you as His bride. Going through the loss of a loved one? He has a plan, and He says that anyone who believes in Him will never die. The theme of our lives is that God will never be tricked, taken aback, or blindsided by anything that happens to us. He has a plan in all things, especially in the lives of His children.

Walk a different path. Our questions about the future may seem scary, but God has answered all our concerns through the promise of His good plans for us.

#walkadifferentpath

Walk a different path.

I received a call from the school yesterday, letting me know that Connor was sick. I couldn't go pick him up right away, but when I could, I drove to get him as fast as I could so I could bring him home with me. We got home, I gave him some medicine, and he lay down on the couch. I told him his bed would probably be better, but he said he wanted to be close to my office area where I was. I let him sleep with me that night so I could keep an eye on him, and I remember watching him while he slept, love welling up in my heart and tears filling my eyes at this beautiful little boy whom I get to call my son. Out loud, I said to Renae that I couldn't believe he would be ten this year, and my tears continued—not because of sadness, but out of the sheer beauty of being his dad and wanting to protect and care for him because I love him.

As much as I love my kids, my feelings pale in comparison to the love that God has for them and for each of us. Our Father longs to have a loving relationship with each and every one of us, simply because of His great love for His children. His Word states that He has loved us with an everlasting love (see Jeremiah 31:3), meaning that His love for us stretches beyond any amount of time and space, infinitely reaching out constantly and pulling us to Him. While I would lay down my very life for my kids, God has proven that He would sacrifice anything just to be with us, and not because He had to, but because His love for us compelled Him to. The cross of Calvary is the ultimate display of love to us in that it reveals the true heart of our loving Creator, One who would rather die than spend eternity without us. Jesus' death built the bridge to that love and allows us to enter into the place of infinite love with the knowledge that we are worth everything to Him.

Walk a different path. Our love for our children is special in His eyes, but we know that we are also special to Him just because we are His.

#walkadifferentpath

Walk a different path.

Years ago, Renae and I decided to turn the garage into a game room/office and put in a fake wall rather than sealing up the garage. When you walked into the garage, you would never know that the wall was fake by looking at it, as by design, it was made to look like an original part of the house. How many of us have those moments when we put up fake smiles instead of walls? We smile even though we are struggling on the inside, whether it be from financial struggles, rejection, or heartbreak. We are soldiering through life, hiding behind a fake smile, telling everyone that we are fine, when really, inside, we are dying a little each day. The pain of uncertainty, feeling unloved, or losing someone we love eats away at us and leaves us feeling used up and hopeless, but yet we still flash the smile to not let anyone see the true pain we are hiding.

No one is exempt from pain and heartbreak, but God did not intend for us to stay in that place of suffering. He knows the trials we go through and how we hide them from the world, yet He calls out to us and beckons us to come to Him, casting all our burdens and pain on Him. God longs to be that Source in your life that provides for your needs daily, that will never reject you, and that mends the shattered pieces of your broken heart. He will turn our mourning to dancing (see Psalm 30:11) and our sadness to joy if we surrender to Him and allow His loving hands to mold us and lead us down the path for His name's sake. We must always remember that no eye has seen, no ear has heard, and no mind has imagined the things God has prepared for those who love Him (see 1 Corinthians 2:9).

Walk a different path. Fake smiles can fool the world, but God longs to wipe our tears and restore a happy heart within to make us smile again.

#walkadifferentpath

Walk a different path.

I had a pretty interesting discussion with Matthew as we ate an early lunch today. He was telling me he had a crush on a little girl at school—a different one from the one he'd told me about a month ago. He proceeded to tell me she didn't like him, that none of the girls he liked felt the same way about him. I told him he was just eight years old and he didn't need to worry about that right now, but I understand how he felt because his daddy has gone through that, as well. Once again, he is young and has plenty of time to worry about finding a girlfriend, but I know that in life, we can all feel the way he did. We want to be liked and have our feelings and interest returned; we want to feel that we are wanted, valued, and especially, loved.

While it may seem cliché, there is Someone who really does love you. Not only does He love you, but He likes you, as well! God likes you so much that He wants to spend time with you, hear your thoughts on things, and make you feel wanted and loved. God wants to be your best Friend, your number-one Confidant, and the Person you depend on when all seems to be falling apart. Jesus died to show you how much He loves you, and He rose again to show you that you don't have to be afraid, because He has your back and is the best Friend you could hope for (see 1 Peter 5:7).

Walk a different path. Some people may not like you, but God likes you enough to love you and give everything to be with you.

#walkadifferentpath

Walk a different path.

Oh, those twin brothers. How they love to come in and make a mess of our lives! One sets you up, and the other comes in and knocks you down. Who are these two troublemakers, and why do we let them rule so many aspects of our lives? Anxiety and fear just love to wreak havoc in our minds and hearts. Anxiety causes you to worry about what will happen in your job, whether your kids are alright, or whether you will be alone forever, and then fear swoops in and drives its claws right into the exposed part of you that anxiety opened up. These two are a formidable tag team, and they long to break us down to the point that we are worried about everything and fearful of what we will lose in life.

The words "be anxious for nothing" (Philippians 4:6 NKJV) and "do not fear" (see Isaiah 44:8; Matthew 10:31) are both frequently found in the Word—and for good reason. God understands that we may look at our life situations and worry about the outcomes, but He has told us not to be anxious about anything. He wants us to present our worries to Him so that He can guard our hearts and minds. He also knows there is no need to fear because He will go before us and fight the battles that we cannot see. See, our Father wants to give us a life free of anxiety and fear, a life that is fruitful and complete in Him, free from the despair that worry brings.

Walk a different path. Let not your heart be troubled because God is your strong tower, and fear and anxiety are not allowed in where He is present.

#walkadifferentpath

Walk a different path.

Happy Valentine's Day! We will hear those words a lot today. It is such a beautiful holiday in some ways, because I believe it brings out the romantic feelings in both women and men. The ladies will get the flowers, boxes of candy, jewelry, and romantic dinners they deserve, and the men will get the privilege of being with the beautiful women who have captured their hearts. Love will be in the air, and people will tend to be a little nicer—sort of like at Christmastime—and things don't seem so bad in the world.

While all this is great, there is a romance that stretches as far as the eye can see, deeper than any depth known to man. This romance is the love story that is being written about you and God. Throughout all of time, there has never been a story that carries so much love and commitment as the one our Creator is writing with each and every one of us. All of heaven rejoices when we come to know Him (see Luke 15:7), and He continues to pursue us and protect us, showing us a love that is greater than any other that has been. If you need proof, just look at the cross of Calvary. He would rather die than not be with you, and He is always reaching out and calling to you, longing to be the love of your life.

Walk a different path. Valentine's gifts and gestures are great, but God's words, "I am my beloved's, and my beloved is mine," reminds us that we are His eternally (Song of Solomon 6:3 NKJV).

#walkadifferentpath

Walk a different path.

The day after. So many feelings are tied up in those three little words. Think about it: there are some great and happy moments and memories we experience *the day after.* Waking up and looking outside to see that new car in the driveway, or waking up after a long flight to find you are on a beach in Hawaii, or waking up the next day to remember you are a new dad or mom for the first time. All these life-altering days are amazing, and they fill us with hope and joy. However, there are some not-so-good "day afters," as well. The day after finding out your job is relocating overseas, the day after you waited for that person to text or call and they never did, or even worse, the day after you lost that special person in your life. "Day afters" can be good or bad, and they can come out of nowhere, leaving us as high as a kite, or blindsided like we've been hit by a train.

Still, God is the King of today—and all the days after. He is there cheering for us when we get the opportunity to buy the new car, or go on that much-needed vacation, and especially when we our children are born. He is also there holding our hearts and whispering in our ears that He will never leave us when the job does go away, reminding us that He will provide. He is there for us when that person didn't reach out and call, telling us He always wants to spend time with us. And God will be there when tragedy strikes, because He understands loss and He wants to comfort our hearts and hold us close to Him when we are broken inside. God "is the same yesterday, today, and forever" (Hebrews 13:8 NKJV), and we can rest in the knowledge that He will constantly work for our benefit, providing us with what we need, even if it's sometimes not what we want.

Walk a different path. God is the King of the universe, but His greatest desire is to be with you for every "day after" you have.

#walkadifferentpath

Walk a different path.

"I can't wait until the weekend." "I can't wait to see you." "I can't wait to go on vacation." What are the words of the old song—the "waiting is the hardest part"? Face it, my friend, none of us likes to wait. It is difficult for us to wait on even the simplest things, to the point that it can drive us nuts and even put us in a bad mood. Waiting, waiting, waiting—it seems to go on and on. I know for a fact that I struggle with this at times, feeling like I am missing out on things because they don't seem to come to me when I want them, or worse, when something I *don't* want comes because I didn't wait.

The Bible mentions many stories about waiting. Abraham and Sarah waited twenty-five years for the promise of Isaac to be fulfilled. The Israelites waited forty years to enter the Promised Land. David waited fifteen years to be king. One famous verse of Scripture tells us, "*They that wait upon the* Lord *shall renew their strength*" (Isaiah 40:31 kjv). The theme here is *waiting*, which God knows is hard for us, but He allows us to wait because He can see down the road of life, and He wants what is best for us, not just what we want. He teaches us to wait so we can receive the blessing He has so lovingly prepared for us, in the timing when it is needed and when it will make the most positive impact on our lives.

Walk a different path. No one likes to wait, but waiting on Him will ensure that what we receive is better than our minds can comprehend.

#walkadifferentpath

Walk a different path.

When I recently had my hair cut, the stylist asked me about the kids. She commented about how Chloe is outnumbered at the house as she is the only girl. That word, *outnumbered*, really stuck with me—because she was right. Chloe has been living with all males in the house since her mom has been gone. It also got me thinking about how each of us can feel like we are outnumbered in our daily lives, as well. Deadlines at work seem to pile up, pushing at us until we feel overwhelmed. Trying to meet new people and make new connections can have us feeling outnumbered, as well, because so many bad experiences on both sides have piled up against us, making it difficult to break through and establish a real bond with a new person. We can also feel outnumbered by the sheer weight of what is happening in our world, where right seems to take a backseat and going with the flow, even if it isn't God's way, seems to be the answer to avoiding conflict.

God is never outmaneuvered, and He certainly is never outnumbered. The Word states in the book Psalms that "a thousand may fall at your side, ten thousand at your right hand, but it will not come near you" (Psalm 91:7 NIV). The psalmist was speaking about David, but I believe God wants us to see the verse as a blueprint for our everyday lives, as well, in that we are never outnumbered because our Father never is. God goes before us and springs the traps of fear, anxiety, and worry, showing us that the things that seem to hold weight in our lives are really just stepping-stones on the path to a life fulfilled in Him, free of unwarranted concerns. The Bible tells us that *"the angel of the LORD encamps around us those who fear him, and he delivers them"* (Psalm 34:7 NIV), regardless of the number of enemies that seem to be around us.

Walk a different path. Feeling outnumbered does not have to be our reality when we have a God who swings the battle always in our favor.

#walkadifferentpath

Walk a different path.

It is so beautiful how it happens. A child, a parent, a significant other—all of them stir this feeling in us. When my kids were born, I immediately fell in love, and that love grows more and more each day. I miss my mom, and still, to this day, I love her as much as I can remember when I first felt that love toward her years ago when I was a kid. I look at my dad and just know I love him without a shred of doubt. I miss Renae, but the love I had for her remains forever in my heart and allows me to believe in another day when I will be able to share a romantic love with someone else. To love and to be in love are so closely related, and they both instill in us the belief that there is a better world and that there is no price too high to pay to share that love with others.

Now, take all the love you can remember and multiply it times infinity, and you still will not come close to the love God has for each and every one of us. We are His children, and He loves us unconditionally—just because we are His. He loves us like a Father in that He provides for us and seeks to protect us from anything that would cause us harm, gently speaking to us to show us a better way. God is the best Significant Other in our lives, as well, because He is so in love with each and every one of us, and like a good partner, He is jealous and will not share us with anyone else, because we are His. God loves us all, but more importantly, He is madly in love with us, and you only have to look toward Calvary to see the immeasurable love He has poured out for us.

Walk a different path. Love is eternal in our hearts, and with God, that eternal love can save any soul (see 1 John 4:8).

#walkadifferentpath